IT HAPPENED IN OKLAHOMA

It Happened In Series

IT HAPPENED IN
OKLAHOMA

Robert L. Dorman

TWODOT®

GUILFORD, CONNECTICUT
HELENA, MONTANA
AN IMPRINT OF THE GLOBE PEQUOT PRESS

A · **TWODOT**® · **BOOK**

Copyright © 2006 by Morris Book Publishing, LLC

Text design: Nancy Freeborn
Map by M. A. Dubé © Morris Book Publishing, LLC
Front cover: Oklahoma settlers in front of their dugout, Library of Congress Prints and Photographs Division, LC-USZ62-100337
Back cover: Geronimo's Last Buffalo, Library of Congress Prints and Photographs Division, LC-USZ62-127717

Library of Congress Cataloging-in-Publication Data
Dorman, Robert L.
  It happened in Oklahoma / Robert L. Dorman.— 1st ed.
     p. cm.
  Includes bibliographical references and index.
  ISBN 978-0-7627-4000-0 (alk. paper)
  1. Oklahoma—History—Anecdotes. I. Title.
  F694.6.D67 2005
  976.6—dc22
                                        2006013084

Manufactured in the United States of America
First Edition/Third Printing

CONTENTS

CONTENTS

PREFACE

Oklahoma defies easy labels and preconceptions. It is not especially flat, treeless, or dusty. It is not particularly rural, backwards, or quaint. It has a number of large lakes, none of which is natural. Churchgoing is popular there, and so is gambling and divorce. Oklahoma is the fast-food capital of America, and it is home to a prestigious international literary prize.

Oklahoma's history is surprising and never boring. At least five great historical dramas have happened there: the Trail of Tears, the land runs, the Tulsa Race Riot, the Dust Bowl, and the Oklahoma City bombing. These events transcend time and place in their compelling human interest. Everything else that occurred in between is merely fascinating.

In some ways Oklahoma and its history are like that of a southern state; in other ways it is more midwestern, and in still other respects, western. Slavery and Civil War battles share the same landscape as sod houses, tornadoes, Indian wars, and cattle drives. Oklahoma history may be shorter than that of some other states, but it is history on "fast-forward."

It Happened in Oklahoma tells the story of the big events and the small ones that made the state what it is today. Although admitted to the union as recently as 1907, Oklahoma is not as young as it seems. It possesses a deep and rich Native American history that far predates Columbus—and Christ, for that matter. Its modern history began with the Indian removals that occurred in the 1820s and 1830s, culminating with the Trail of Tears. The land runs of the 1890s heralded the end of the Indian republics and the patchwork of reservations that almost seventy different tribes and nations called home. Hundreds of thousands of white settlers poured into Indian Territory and Oklahoma Territory, lured by the promise of homesteads and the discovery of oil. When Oklahoma was formed out of the Twin Territories in 1907, it was the fastest-growing state in the nation, larger in population than many established states. In the decades following, Oklahoma endured a succession of booms and busts, never quite relinquishing the frontier mindset. Since the last oil bust of the 1980s, a new maturity seems to have come to the state, a desire to plan and build for the long-term.

Oklahoma is an unexpectedly beautiful state, and its people are genuinely friendly. Of course, I write these words with a certain bias—my family has lived in the same small Oklahoma town for over a hundred years. I wish to thank my wife, Sarah, for all of her support throughout the writing of this book, which benefited greatly from her critic's eye. I would like to dedicate *It Happened in Oklahoma* to my son, whose namesake, his great-great-grandfather Hubert Dorman, was a frontiersman and government interpreter who lived among the Kickapoo, Sac, and Fox, and other tribes in Indian Territory, and who later helped to found the community of Jones, Oklahoma, my hometown.

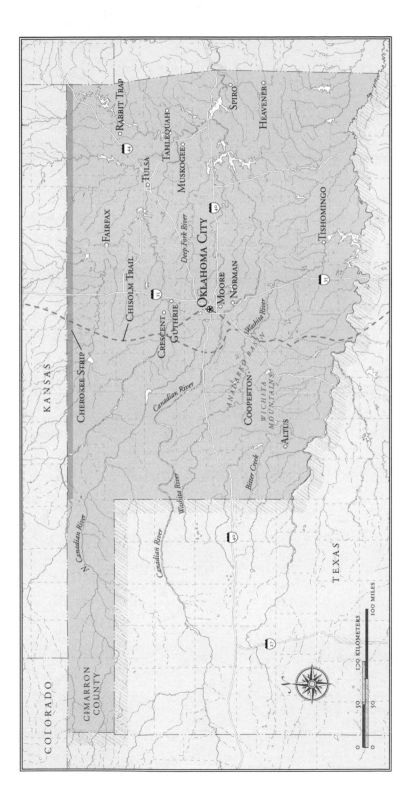

OKLAHOMA

OLD PAINT

- 8,OOO B.C. -

Harper County

IT WAS APRIL 15, 1993—the first day of turkey season—and Leland Bement and a colleague from the state archaeological survey were returning to a location that they already knew to be the site of a bison kill. Hundreds of bones at the site had gradually been exposed over the years by rain and erosion. But just how old the site was, no one knew. The archaeologists were following the footprints of numerous turkey hunters up to the bluff, where the bones protruded from the soil. There they found that one of the hunters had pulled a few of the bones free, causing the stone tip of a spear-point to come into plain view. When they saw that spear-point, the two scientists knew that the site would require much more investigation. The spear-point had been carved by the Folsom people, who had lived over 10,000 years ago and are ancient ancestors of today's Native Americans.

On its own, such a find would have designated the bison bonebed, known as the Cooper site, as a significant discovery. Folsom sites are rare finds; only one other had been identified in Oklahoma up to that time. But the real treasure of the Cooper site was yet to be revealed.

During the preliminary excavation over the next month, the painstaking work of the scientists and volunteers was interrupted by Oklahoma's infamous stormy weather. A tornado passed overhead, along with torrential rain and, worse, baseball-sized hail. Many of the top layers of bison bones were pounded to bits. Other bones were knocked away from their carefully noted positions. Still others were reburied in mud and required excavation all over again. The scientists and volunteers set back to work, securing and protecting the site for future investigations.

Excavation resumed in the spring and summer of 1994. Bement and others determined that in fact three bison kills had occurred at the gully at different times. The bison were not the familiar buffalo known today, but were of an extinct species, *Bison antiquus,* which were substantially larger and had massive straight horns jutting from the sides of their heads. The richness of the bone deposit, coupled with the evidence that multiple kills had been staged in the ancient gully, were enough for the scientists to conclude that they had found something special. Then, after several more months of hot and dusty work, the Cooper site gave up its fabulous secret.

It was July 11, 1994. Bement was at the site, cleaning dirt off of a leg bone, and beneath it he could see the eye sockets of a skull. When he lifted the leg away, he was struck dumb, and the rest of his co-workers fell silent: there, painted on the frontal portion of the skull, was a bright red zigzag, like a lightning bolt. This simple marking is the oldest painted artwork ever discovered in North America.

Bement and his colleagues have subsequently examined the painted skull using a scanning electron microscope and other sophisticated equipment. The paint, they found, was made of hematite, a common mineral on the southern plains. They have tried to reconstruct exactly what happened in that northwestern Oklahoma gully over ten millennia ago, and what the meaning of the painted skull might have been. They knew from previous studies that the Folsom people were nomadic, traveling in small bands and following the bison herds across the plains region. The materials for their spear-points were taken from far-flung locations in what are now Texas and Kansas. The Folsom hunters shared the landscape not only with the super-sized bison, but also with mammoths, giant sloths, and other animals.

Before the Cooper site excavations, little had been uncovered regarding the social life and culture of the Folsom people. The repeated use of the gully for bison kills indicated some degree of planning, forethought, and coordination. More than one group of hunters had to be involved; some needed to drive the bison into the gully, while others posted themselves along the rim with their spears poised for the kill. After the deed was done, many hands were required to strip meat from the skeletons of such a large number of animals. The scrapes of stone knives are still visible on some of the bones.

The three kills at the Cooper site occurred several years apart, yet always during the late summer and early fall season. The skull that was later decorated seems to belong to the earliest kill, lying long enough for sun, insects, and weather to dry and bleach it. When the Folsom hunters returned to the gully several years after their first successful kill, they retrieved the skull from the pile of remains while making their preparations for the next attempt. The red paint or its ingredients must have been carried from elsewhere. Someone, possibly a shaman or holy person, drew the lightning bolt—a symbol of power—onto the skull, and aimed it in the direction of the gully from which the bison would be driven. Most probably the painted skull was a talisman to lure bison and bring bounty to the people.

Apparently, it worked. Many of the bones in the layer containing the special skull show signs of being trampled by the hooves of the next herd of bison that fell atop them. The special skull itself was broken up, as perhaps was intended by its makers, because they left it where it lay to be trampled in future kills. Over the centuries the nearby Beaver River flooded and changed its course countless times, gradually burying the bones, and that wondrous fragment, under layers of silt and wind-blown sand. Little could its makers have imagined that their handiwork, created for momentary purposes, might retain a power of sorts after thousands of years: the power to communicate something of themselves to another people in the far-distant future.

RUNE OR RUSE?

Heavener

OKLAHOMA IN THE TIME BEFORE COLUMBUS appears to have been a busy place. There are claims that early Chinese explorers may have left behind a statue near Luther. What appears to be the stone floor of an ancient Mayan temple was unearthed south of Edmond. And various rune-stones have been found across the state, from Tulsa to Shawnee, dated by one scholar to a thirteen-year period—in the eleventh century. That the inscriptions on the Heavener Runestone came from the hand of humankind and not from raindrops or squirrels is about all that can be concluded with any certainty. After debate and evidence have been exhausted, there still remains a mystery as immovable as the rock itself: who was responsible for those strange engravings up on Poteau Mountain?

Of course, we do know for certain that eastern Oklahoma in the eleventh century was extensively populated by Native Americans.

Heavener itself is not far from the famous Spiro Mounds, which was a wealthy capital of the Caddoan people and a center for trade along the Arkansas River. Is it not possible that the builders of Spiro, or some other Native Americans, are responsible for the inscriptions? Indeed, the rune-stone at Heavener was known locally as "Indian Rock." It should be remembered that there was a time when American Indians had been deemed incapable of building the mounds that dot the eastern United States; it was assumed that some unknown, more "advanced" people must have been responsible.

So, too, the rune-stones, especially the one at Heavener, came to have their extravagant theories. Most accounts trace knowledge of the site to the Choctaw Indians in the nineteenth century, though actual documentation seems to be scarce. The story resumes with a white hunter named King, who reportedly saw the markings in 1874. Other reports date to the turn-of-the-century and afterward. The most significant being that of Carl Kemmerer, who rediscovered the stone in 1913 and later sent reproductions of the odd symbols to the Smithsonian Institution. According to the standard account, the Smithsonian identified the markings as Norse (or Viking) runes.

Enter Gloria Farley, who has been perhaps the person most responsible for promoting the theory that Viking explorers authored the inscriptions. A native of Heavener, Farley first visited the site as a young girl, with Kemmerer and his daughter in 1928. Farley recalls being impressed by the beautiful setting of the huge stone, which stands twelve feet high and ten feet wide in a deep ravine. The markings are chest-high to an adult and each is about eight inches long. Kemmerer lifted Farley to the top of the rock and allowed her to peer down at it. The vivid experience returned to her many years later when she read about the Kensington Rune Stone of Minnesota. She had married and moved out of state by then, but when she and her family came back to the Heavener area in 1950, Farley decided to revisit the stone at her first opportunity. When she found it again in early 1951, she dubbed it the Heavener Runestone.

Over the next four decades, Farley made it her business to prove the Viking origins of the inscriptions. She interviewed the locals, gathered sworn statements, and corresponded with scholars of alleged Norse exploration in America. Meetings of experts were convened in her living room, where it was decided that the markings could not be of Native American origin. By 1970, Farley's efforts at last began to bear fruit, and, with the help of a state senator, Heavener Runestone State Park was established to protect the site.

Farley's case for the park was bolstered by the findings of a retired army cryptographer named Alf Mongé, who published *Norse Medieval Cryptography in Runic Carvings* with a colleague in 1967. Mongé considered the Heavener stone to be among the most significant artifacts of supposed Norse exploration in mid-continent America. He determined that the symbols were a "cryptopuzzle" that, when decoded, represented the date November 11, 1012. He did the same analysis for several other rune-stones from around the state, determining that they dated from 1009 to 1022. Since the Heavener date coincided with a day of the religious calendar, Mongé's co-author, O. G. Landsverk, concluded that the carver of the inscriptions might have been a priest.

Most professional archaeologists and Scandinavian scholars remained skeptical of such claims. Landsverk himself pointed to a serious weakness in them: he expected that there would be more evidence of Norsemen in Oklahoma (such as graves, weapons, and dwelling-sites), but none has ever been found. The case for Heavener's origins was not helped when scholars began to cast doubt on the authorship of the equally famous Kensington Rune Stone, raising the probability that it might be a hoax perpetrated by an immigrant Scandinavian farmer in the late nineteenth century.

Gloria Farley kept the faith, however, and her patience was rewarded with more scholarly reinforcements during the 1980s. Richard Nielsen, described as an engineer and expert in Norse languages, published a series of articles that strove to re-authenticate the Kensington Rune Stone and to provide a new translation for the Heavener inscriptions. Nielsen believed that the runes should be read as *GLOMEDAL,* which means *Glome's Valley.* An individual named Glome appears to have been staking a claim to the surrounding countryside, with the stone as a giant marker. Startlingly, Nielsen placed the carving still further into the past, somewhere around the year A.D. 750.

Farley, who has written her own book on pre-Columbian oddities in America, leans toward Nielsen's conclusions. She rejected outright a more recent, alternative theory of the meaning of the runes. According to a Sallisaw minister, Dr. Lee W. Woodard, the runestone was created in 1687 by one of the associates of the French explorer La Salle, who allegedly died in the vicinity. The markings represent a monument to La Salle and his expedition.

All such theories regarding the origins of the Heavener Runestone continue to be just intriguing enough, and just inconclusive enough, to perpetuate interest in the site. In 2003 the state tourism commission agreed to allow an investigation of a collapsed cave nearby, where it was hoped more runes or some artifacts might finally be found, but none have been reported. Two European experts arrived in that same year with ultraviolet lights in hand, which they used to examine the markings in an attempt to confirm their age; however, their results were inconclusive.

In her response to Dr. Woodard's theory attributing the runes to a La Salle compatriot, Gloria Farley noted a feature of the inscriptions that is rarely mentioned, but which might entail a theory all its own: there are two initials in English, "E. S.," close to the rightmost rune. The artist's signature? Who can say? But it leads to what may be the most provocative theory of all: that the inscriptions may mean nothing; they may be mere random carvings set in stone, collecting theories.

THAT FATAL COUNTRY

- 1834 -

Fort Gibson

"I HAVE BECOME SO MUCH INDIAN OF LATE," the artist George Catlin wrote home from Fort Gibson in June 1834, "that my pencil has lost all appetite for subjects that savour of tameness." It was the eve of his departure with the Leavenworth-Dodge Expedition, and he was still full of the fervor that had driven him up and down the frontier for the past three years, sketching portraits and landscapes of Native American life. He called his wide-ranging travels a "true School of the Arts," more valuable to him than a lifetime spent in New York studios. His only concern about the upcoming expedition—the first-ever foray of nearly 500 soldiers, guides, and scouts into the lands of the Comanches and Wichitas—was that the show of force might "frighten them out of *sketching distance.*"

Catlin would need all of this enthusiasm and more to sustain him during the harrowing journey that lay ahead. The expedition was intended both to impress the western plains tribes and to establish formal relations with them. Congress had passed legislation for Indian removal in the East, and the army was charged with reconnoitering future areas of settlement and relocation. Among the hundreds of men who set out with Catlin on June 20 under the command of General Henry Leavenworth were two others who would later join Catlin in the annals of future fame: Jefferson Davis, then a youngish lieutenant in the U.S. Army, and Jesse Chisholm, already working as a pathfinder on the plains.

When it began, the Leavenworth-Dodge Expedition was an imposing array of mounted soldiers, guides from diverse tribes, supply wagons, and dozens of cattle to feed the troops. Leavenworth initially pushed southwestward from Fort Gibson and crossed the Canadian River on June 25, averaging about 20 miles per day. By the first of July, the men had made it to the vicinity of the mouth of the Washita River where it meets the Red River.

Catlin was entranced by the scenery before him—the timberland that alternated with rolling prairie, dotted with buffalo—and declared it "a panorama too beautiful to be painted with a pen." He found wild grapes that were delicious, and he eagerly joined in a buffalo hunt. Yet Catlin was too experienced a frontier traveler to think that the trip to the west and back would be easy. "[O]ne thing is certain . . . we shall meet with many severe privations and reach that place a jaded set of fellows," he wrote.

Catlin's qualms proved to be true all too quickly. Even before they left the camp on the Washita, a strange illness began to strike both men and beasts alike. Three officers, including General Leavenworth himself, along with forty-five soldiers and seventy-five horses and mules, were the first to be stricken with the terrible fever, which was made worse by the oppressive summer heat. Temperatures reached as high as 107 degrees, intolerable to men in wool uniforms. As each day passed, more men fell ill. By July 3 rafts had been built to cross the deep brown waters of the Washita, and Independence Day was marked on the opposite bank. It was decided that Colonel Dodge, the second in command, would continue on with the able-bodied troops, while the general would recuperate with the rest and bring up the rear with some of the supply wagons. As it turned out, however, Leavenworth died within days after the expedition departed.

The expedition that now pushed westward numbered about 250 men, so great had the toll of the sickness been; some had died, many more were incapacitated, and others remained behind to care for the sick. The expedition was no longer an overwhelming force, and the soldiers were edgy as they ventured farther into unknown Indian lands. In the dead of night on July 7, a sentry mistook a stray horse for an attacker and shot it through the heart, alarming the whole camp and stampeding their horse herd in the process. Much of the following day was spent recovering the horses.

About a hundred miles out from the Washita camp, Colonel Dodge and his men at last encountered a party of Comanches, who were wary at first, but finally agreed to accompany the expedition to a large village near the Wichita Mountains. En route, Catlin was amazed at the teeming numbers of bison and wild horses. He and a friend attempted to catch a mustang by "creasing" it with a rifle— shooting it through the gristle on top of its neck and thus stunning it. They had seen marksmen do it before, but their own shooting skills were not up to the task, and they were grieved when they broke the horse's neck.

On July 16, Catlin was greatly relieved to reach camp near the Comanche village, a busy place of hundreds of lodges. He wrote happily, "I am with subjects rude and almost infinite around me, for my pen and my brush." Catlin marveled at the horsemanship of the Comanches, pronouncing them the best he had ever seen. The soldiers were on good terms with their hosts, who looked upon the white men with great curiosity—"as if we had come from the moon," Catlin remarked. Within days, though, the sickness hit Catlin along with more than two dozen others. Around this time, a Comanche warrior took a liking to Catlin's old, worn umbrella and brought better and better horses in hopes of a trade. Ordinarily the artist would have been glad to barter for artifacts, but the feverish Catlin could not part with the device, which he used to shield himself from the sun. The Comanche later found an army officer only too happy to swap a cheap umbrella for a fine horse.

Catlin and about thirty other sick men and an equal number of guards and caregivers were left in a makeshift fort outside the Comanche village, while Dodge limped on with the remainder of the expedition to parley with the Wichitas, Pawnees, and Kiowas farther to the west. By most accounts, Dodge was a diplomatic success in his meetings with the plains tribes. But the lurking sickness made time pressing, as did depleted rations, and presently he gathered his "pitiful little encampment," as Catlin described it, and turned his men back toward Fort Gibson and into a deepening drought.

Now the expedition truly was racing against time. Their progress was slowed by the dozens of litters, carrying the sick and dying, that they dragged behind them. They had very little food, and there was no game to be found and no drinkable water. The relentless sun had dried up the grass so that the horses were starving as well. Catlin recalled that "sometimes for the distance of many miles, the only water we could find, was in stagnant pools . . . in which the buffaloes have been lying and wallowing like hogs in a mud-puddle." Here the horses "irresistibly ran and plunged their noses, sucking up the dirty and poisonous draught, until, in some instances, they fell dead in their tracks."

After six days, the expedition finally met with some good fortune when it reached the banks of the sandy Canadian River, where buffalo abounded. There was still little good water, and the sickness would not release its grip. Catlin was delirious for much of the return trip, riding in the back of a supply wagon, where he was jostled so harshly that the skin of his elbows and knees was worn off. At last, on August 15, Colonel Dodge and what was left of his men stumbled to the bank of the Arkansas River, opposite Fort Gibson.

As many as 150 men died during the Leavenworth-Dodge Expedition, and a greater number fell ill from the mysterious fever. As for George Catlin, he recuperated at Fort Gibson for several weeks, where he listened with dread to the daily funeral services for those less lucky. Finally he could take no more, and against the advice of his doctors, he packed up his sketchbook and other belongings, and resolved to put as much distance as he could between himself and "that fatal country" which was so important to his art.

AFTER THE TEARS

- 1846 -

Tahlequah

THE STORY OF THE CHEROKEE TRAIL OF TEARS has been told many times, and rightly so: It was one of the most important, and shameful, episodes in all of American history. Yet the story does not end there. What happened to the surviving Cherokees after they reached their destination? Was there life after the Trail of Tears? That story is less well known, and it provides an inspiring counterpoint to the tragedy of Indian removal, a new chapter marked by resilience and endurance.

The losses on the Trail of Tears had been terrible almost beyond imagining. At least 1,500 people had died in the stockades in Georgia while waiting to depart. Another 1,600 or more had perished during the journey due to hunger, disease, and exposure. Successive waves of exiles arrived at the new Cherokee lands in the West during 1838 and 1839. Some required two months to cover the 800 miles, while others took as long as four months because of the harsh conditions. More people died in the months immediately after arrival, struck by disease and shorted on rations by corrupt government contractors.

Those first months were among the hardest that the Cherokees had to face in their new territory. To survive, they were forced to fall back on some of their ancestral ways. Supplies were so scarce that many did not have bowls and pots or simple utensils with which to eat. In their previous existence back east, these items were available for sale or barter at stores and trading posts; but now most Cherokees were so poor that they had no money and nothing to trade. Tribal elders remembered how to make clay pots for cooking and holding water. They carved spoons out of wood, and made shoes and clothing out of animal hides. In addition, the government had confiscated their firearms, so for a time the Cherokees had to employ bows and arrows for hunting in order to put meat on the table.

There were many other adjustments that had to be made in order to adapt to their new home. Soils and climate were different from what they were accustomed to. Many of the best parcels of land were already taken by earlier Cherokee emigrants, and the 1839 newcomers had to make do with more marginal areas. Some found it difficult to adapt and sought solace in alcohol, or resorted to crime. But most struggled on and worked constantly to rebuild their lives.

Unfortunately, one aspect of Cherokee society that survived the Trail of Tears intact was the old tribal animosities. The recriminations over the removal treaty continued for years to come, the tribe still split between those who had opposed the treaty and those who had consented. Several prominent signers of the treaty, including Elias Boudinot and John Ridge, were assassinated as traitors by members of the anti-treaty John Ross faction. The Treaty Party mobilized for revenge, with a view of ultimately overthrowing Ross as chief of the Cherokees. Many of the so-called Old Settlers, who had preceded the other two groups to the West, also resented John Ross and his rule.

It took all of Ross's political skills to try to reconcile these differences and bring some semblance of unity and stability back to Cherokee life. A milestone in this effort was the Treaty of 1846, in which the Ross party agreed finally to accept the terms of the 1835 removal treaty that they had reviled, and to share the federal payment for their former lands among all factions of the tribe. Amnesty was also granted to Treaty Party renegades, who now agreed to accept Ross's leadership. Ross saw the 1846 treaty as an assertion of Cherokee independence and national unity. For ordinary Cherokees, it meant they would finally receive their long-delayed and much-needed compensation for removal.

Such money was important to the continuing struggle to rebuild the Cherokees' economy and social fabric. By the 1850s, they had made remarkable progress in this direction. The Cherokee population, according to best estimates, was about 14,000 in 1851 (still down from 16,500 in 1835); by 1860, the number had risen to 22,000. A public school system was established with more than two dozen schools. Seminaries for both men and women were created for the training of teachers, with professors drawn from the best universities in the East. In Tahlequah, the capital of the Cherokee Nation, there were government buildings including a supreme court, five hotels, numerous law offices, stores, and a brick Masonic temple. A bilingual newspaper, the *Cherokee Advocate,* was also published in Tahlequah. In nearby Park Hill, one could see the fine residences and carriages of the half-blood Cherokee elite. Throughout the Cherokee Nation, there were similar signs of social and economic advancement—dozens of blacksmith shops, sawmills and gristmills, and cattle, hogs, and horses in the tens of thousands. Steamboats ran up and down the Arkansas, carrying cotton and other trade goods to the Mississippi and the larger world beyond.

Yet the unity and stability of the Cherokee Nation was always fragile at best, and tragically, in establishing their new nation, the Cherokees made the same mistake as America's founding fathers. They accommodated a great social and political evil, slavery, which ultimately would tear their nation apart once again, just as it shattered the Union. Slaves had helped the Cherokees rebuild quickly, and by 1860 there were about 4,000 in the Nation. Only 10 percent of Cherokees owned slaves, which caused another division in their society, between slaveholders and non-slaveholders. Combined with the longstanding divide between full-bloods and half-bloods, and the old division between the Ross Party and the Treaty Party, the issues of slavery and secession split the Nation asunder in 1861. Siding with the Confederacy, the Cherokee government made a poor bargain.

Much of what the Cherokees had built since 1839 was laid to waste over the next four years of the Civil War. Their population was decimated, as they were hit hard by disease, starvation, and marauding guerillas. When the war was over, the Cherokees, along with the other nations of the so-called Five Civilized Tribes, were punished more severely than any former Confederate state. What would the Cherokee people do now?

They began to rebuild their society once more.

A SECOND TRAIL OF TEARS

- 1861 -

Chustenahlah

CHIEF OPOTHLEYAHOLA OF THE CREEK NATION WAS NO SAINT. He owned a plantation and a large number of slaves. He was not above politics, and was reputed to be among the wealthiest men in the Indian Territory. There are even legends that several of Opothleya-hola's slaves were killed to protect the secret of his buried treasure, a large stash of gold coins that had been sent by the federal government. Yet Opothleyahola's leadership of the Loyal Creeks and other refugees on their flight to Kansas—one of the most tragic and heartrending episodes of the Civil War—was also one of the shining moments of his long career.

There were, to be sure, very few saints to be found in the Indian Territory or elsewhere during the Civil War era. As was true of the rest of the country, the Indian nations divided against themselves, and the animosities that were aroused could be appalling. Out of no particular fondness for the slaves, but with painful memories of the Creeks' ejection from the southern states of Georgia and Alabama, Opothleyahola became the leader of those who chose to remain loyal to the Union, or hoped at least to stay out of the conflict. In the fall of 1861, he and his followers among the Creeks in effect seceded from the secession, by refusing to be party to the pro-Confederate treaty of the Creek government with the Confederacy. Several thousand Creeks, along with slaves, free blacks, and refugees from other tribes, gathered near the junction of the North Canadian and Deep Fork rivers. On November 5, they formed a long caravan and began to move northward toward Kansas, where they hoped to find sanctuary. Some hoped for the opportunity to join the Union army.

Ten days later, Colonel Douglas H. Cooper and a mounted Confederate force of Cherokees, Choctaws, Chickasaws, Creeks, and Texans arrived at the abandoned riverside campsite. They turned in pursuit, and on November 19, they caught up with Opothleyahola's caravan where it was encamped at Round Mountain, near the Red Fork of the Arkansas. A short and indecisive battle followed, with Opothleyahola's men driving back the Confederates but then breaking off the fight and retreating as darkness fell. When Cooper's forces tried to resume the attack the next morning, they discovered that the loyalists and refugees had left hurriedly in the direction of Bird Creek.

In the days following, word reached Cooper that Opothleyahola might want to discuss peace terms, and the colonel sent Major Pegg with three detachments of full-blood Cherokees to meet with the Creek leader. Instead, owing partly to an eloquent speech by Opothleyahola, during which he reminded the Cherokees of their mutual ties to ancestral homelands in the East, most of the Cherokees defected to fight alongside the Loyal Creeks. The battle was joined again for four hours on December 9 at a place called Caving Banks.

The Creeks wore cornhusks so that they could tell each other apart in the confusion of the fighting. Both sides pulled back as darkness came, but the Confederates nevertheless counted it as a victory. From Opothleyahola's perspective, his people were caught in a small war of attrition, with losses of men, animals, and goods each time the rebels engaged them. His bands could not survive many more such fights. He continued to retreat toward Kansas, and at best he could say that it was still an orderly retreat.

That orderliness ended on December 26, when the decisive battle finally occurred. The Battle of Chustenahlah, as it came to be called, took place north of Tulsey Town, then a Creek village. Colonel James McQueen McIntosh had deployed from Confederate-controlled Fort Gibson with almost 1,400 troops to reinforce Cooper's men, and it was McIntosh who charged into Opothleyahola's camp and completely routed its defenders. Most of the refugees' supplies and belongings were left behind as terrified women and children fled with their men out of the camp, running desperately northward all through the night, into the face of a winter storm. Those whose strength failed them died of exposure, their bodies eaten by wolves. The next morning, adding terror to the icy weather, Confederate units chased down any remaining stragglers.

Even as Opothleyahola's loyalists and refugees reached Walnut Creek in southern Kansas, their hardships were just beginning. They now had almost no food and only scant clothing and shelter to cope with the harsh winter. A doctor reported seeing seven children completely naked although it was the month of February. Opothleyahola himself lived in a makeshift tent that was open on all sides to the freezing wind. Some caught severe frostbite that required amputation, a procedure that became all too common (one hundred amputations were reported among the Creeks alone). As many as 240 Creeks died during that first winter, and the losses were equally heavy among the Seminoles and other tribes who had joined them on their flight to Kansas. More and more refugees continued to struggle toward Kansas, and many died on the way. Estimates vary, but somewhere between 4,000 and 7,000 people eventually crowded the destitute camps.

The Union military command relocated most of the refugees to LeRoy, Kansas, and provided what meager aid it could. Many of the Creek and Seminole men believed that the best solution to the situation was to march southward with Union forces and retake control of their lands so that their families could be supported once again. They got their chance on July 3, 1862, at Locust Grove. There, under the command of Colonel William Weer, they defeated a small Confederate force and captured prisoners and a large amount of supplies. But Union commanders seemed at a loss to decide the next step in their strategy, and withdrew back to Kansas, leaving the Creeks and others to mount guerilla actions in the areas around Fort Gibson largely unsupported. And so the war dragged on in Indian Territory.

Chief Opothleyahola was probably over eighty years old when he attempted to lead his followers to Kansas; he had been a respected leader of his people for more than forty years. He had survived the Creek version of the Trail of Tears in 1836, when some were marched out of Creek lands in Alabama literally wearing chains. But the experience of this second Trail of Tears finally proved to be too much for him, and he died in the camps at LeRoy, Kansas, as did so many others yearning to escape the maelstrom of the war.

THE TRAIL THAT BUILT A KINGDOM

- 1867 -

Chisholm Trail

IN 1864, WHEN JESSE CHISHOLM BEGAN hauling wagonloads of furs, hides, and trade goods back and forth between the Indian Territory and Kansas, little did he know that he was breaking one of the three great trails of the American West. Like the Santa Fe Trail and the Oregon Trail before it, the Chisholm Trail for a moment in time was caught up in the larger currents of history, involving vast fortunes, transcontinental railroads, the movement of millions of livestock, and the lives of the cowboys who dared to work on it.

The trail was as yet little known when, in 1867, Texas cattleman O. O. Wheeler came upon a set of wagon ruts heading away from the North Canadian River toward Kansas. He and his men were driving a herd of 2,400 longhorns to the newly established railhead of Abilene, and they were able to follow what was already a well-worn path, for other traders besides Chisholm had begun using it as well. Soon enough, cattle drivers were calling the entire length of their route, from San Antonio across Indian Territory to the Kansas cow towns, the "Chisholm Trail."

The demand for beef from the growing urban populations in the East and from Europe was one of the historical forces behind the importance of the Chisholm Trail. Another factor was the huge surplus of wild cattle that had grown up in Texas during the Civil War years. How to bring the supply and demand together was solved by the great cattle drives that brought the beef on the hoof to newly built railroad lines like the Kansas Pacific, at Abilene. On October 20, 1867, the first carloads of cattle were shipped from Abilene to the East. Until the mid-1870s, there were stories of drives held up for hours at a time when large herds of buffalo crossed the path. Thus the transformation of Indian trader Jesse Chisholm's wagon road into the Chisholm Trail was a symptom of the passing of the frontier. The economy of the region was developing beyond the era of trading posts and business by the wagonload.

For although there was much that was daring, dangerous, and even romantic about cowboys on cattle drives, they were really engaged in big business, a system of mass production. They called it the Cattle Kingdom. Thirty-five thousand head arrived at Abilene in 1867, the first year; by 1871, that number had grown to 600,000 head. Often there were multiple herds of thousands of cows that had to be spread out from the trail itself so that there was sufficient grass and water for them during the journey. Other trails, like the Great Western, also sprang up during this period to handle the volume, but the Chisholm in its heyday carried an estimated five million cattle and one million horses northward out of Texas between 1867 and 1884.

A cattle drive, at times, was a leisurely affair of grazing and watering, and it usually took two months or more to complete the entire length of the trail, of which 25-35 days were needed to cross from the Red River to the Kansas border. In general a drive could cover a dozen miles in a day and consisted of 2,500 cattle on average—though herds of up to 10,000 were not uncommon. A herd could stretch out for miles and required at least ten cowboys (or *drovers*) and a trail boss to keep it moving in the right direction.

The cattle drives of the Chisholm Trail have become part of the mythology of the West, thanks to pulp novels, movies, and television series. Yet there was some truth to popular depictions of the hazards of the journey, particularly in the Indian Territory. River crossings could be dangerous, for example, especially in periods of high water. Joseph G. McCoy, who was responsible for promoting Abilene as the terminus of the trail, recalled that "milling"—when cattle swimming across a river would bunch together, become disoriented and tired, and finally drown—was always a potential problem. A drive belonging to cattleman Bill Montgomery lost over one hundred cattle and three horses while crossing the flooded North Canadian in 1870. Very often all that a drover could do was swim his mount out to the milling cattle and position himself in the middle of them, hoping that they would follow his lead. More than a few cowboys were swept from their horses while attempting this feat, and when this happened, their best bet, according to McCoy, was to grab hold of the tail of the nearest steer swimming by and be towed to shore!

Besides floods, other forms of severe weather also posed a hazard for cattle drives on the trail. In 1874, at a place called Hell Roaring Creek, more than six dozen horses died in a freak April blizzard. Thunder and lightning, too, were particularly dangerous, not only to riders, but also because they might trigger a stampede. A cowboy named Robert T. Hill was with a cattle drive on the Cimarron River when a thunderstorm caused that very problem. He and another drover were trying to chase down a small stampede and head it off when, in gathering darkness, a lightning bolt struck quite nearby. Hill's horse jolted to a stop, and Hill could see in the flash that his horse had halted scarcely a foot from the edge of a steep drop-off. Hill's friend was less lucky. The lightning had hit and killed a nearby steer, and knocked the man unconscious. Several of the cattle they had been chasing had plunged over the cliff to their deaths.

Indian peoples along the Chisholm Trail were another cause for concern. They believed, not unreasonably, that the drives crossing their lands owed a toll of some sort. Roaming bands tried simply to extort a few head of cattle for themselves under the threat of violence or stampede. When trail boss A. J. Day was confronted by 300 Osage warriors while crossing Indian Territory, he was only too happy to cut out the ten head that they demanded. Another drive gave ten head to what looked like thousands of encamped Comanches; unsatisfied, the Comanches returned at night and stampeded off an additional 250. Another ploy that tribesmen took advantage of was to make off with an outfit's horses after dark, then bring them back the next day to collect a reward. For the most part, though, violence between the cowboys and the Indians was rare, thanks in part to periodic military escorts and to Fort Sill, established in 1869 to help protect the cattle drives.

From a Native American perspective, the frontier must have appeared rather crowded during the heyday of the Chisholm Trail, with massive numbers of animals and men constantly afoot. Soon enough, it would prove too crowded for the cattle drives as well. By the late 1870s and early 1880s, farmers and ranchers were moving into Kansas and Texas and stringing up barbed wire. State quarantine laws, particularly in Kansas, made business more and more difficult. New railroads were built, changing the economic equation that promoted the drives, as did the expansion of the beef industry elsewhere in the West. The Chisholm's endpoint switched several times in response to some of these circumstances, from Abilene to Ellsworth and finally to Caldwell, Kansas, right on the border. Ultimately, the Chisholm Trail was supplanted by the Great Western, but by then, the Cattle Kingdom's days were numbered. The historically bad winter of 1886–87 was the final straw, causing huge losses in the industry and pushing many cattlemen into bankruptcy. Over the decades since then, as grass and trees began once again to grow over the trampled ground and wagon ruts, the Chisholm Trail faded from sight, but not from history.

CUSTER'S DRESS REHEARSAL

- 1868 -

Washita River

CUSTER AND BLACK KETTLE: OF THE TWO, BLACK KETTLE was the more ill fated on that day, November 27, 1868. At council the night before, even as the Seventh Cavalry was drawing into position, he had decided to move his village closer to the thousands of Kiowas, Cheyennes, and Arapahoes who were encamped further down the river. He would move them tomorrow. As it stood, he and his people were off to themselves, exposed, though Black Kettle was not to realize the magnitude of his blunder until it was too late.

Black Kettle was a man of peace. He had implored the commander at Fort Cobb to allow his village to camp nearby for sanctuary, but the commander would have none of it. Black Kettle had to trust in sheer distance and the season of the year for protection. Unfortunately, the era was fast coming to an end when the West would have room enough for retreat. This was the lesson that the peoples gathered along the Washita, particularly the Cheyennes, were already learning.

Black Kettle had survived one massacre, at Sand Creek, Colorado, in 1864, only to come south and have his destiny catch up with him.

Rather than watch their hunting grounds be filled with settlers, some of the younger men of the tribes had taken matters into their own hands. In Kansas, there were attacks, captives, and depredations. The whole state was in a frenzy for revenge. Such an atmosphere had justified General Sheridan in dispatching Custer and the Seventh Cavalry into Indian Territory, to punish and to pacify—to show that there was no refuge anymore.

Custer required no encouragement; he was always keen for a fight. Frankly, too, his career needed a boost. Just over a year earlier, he had been court-martialed and suspended from rank for being absent without leave (to be nearer his beloved wife) and, more seriously, for the summary execution of some deserters from his regiment. General Sheridan had summoned him out of his temporary "retirement" as just the man to undertake an expedition against Black Kettle. Custer did not have to be asked twice.

When the order came, he drove his men hard for three days out of Camp Supply. The terrain was rolling and grassy, interrupted by gullies and buttes. There was deep snow on the ground and the weather was bitter. The conditions did not prevent the flamboyant Custer from bringing along his usual accoutrements, including the regimental band. Yet his dead earnestness was shown by the fact that just before the battle, he—a dog lover—had several of his prize animals killed to prevent their barking and giving up the advantage of surprise. The men spent a long, cold night without benefit of fires and were forbidden to walk around to keep warm.

Custer had decided to divide his command, a dubious idea that he would repeat at Little Bighorn. He planned to attack Black Kettle's village from four directions simultaneously. He would give the signal at dawn. Not long before first light, the troops saw Venus, the morning star, appear out of a fog and mistook it for a warning rocket, fearing that they had been discovered. But the Cheyennes slept on, oblivious. In years to come, Custer was to be known as "Son of the Morning Star," a name that he wore with pride because it recalled this occasion of his only major victory in the Indian wars.

While the regimental band played the jaunty tune "Garry Owen," the Seventh charged into the village. Custer rode a black stallion and, by his own account, killed one Cheyenne on his way to a position from which to oversee the operation. Rumbling between the dozens of lodges, the troopers slashed and shot indiscriminately as men, women, and children emerged into the mayhem and ran for their lives. Some took up arms to offer resistance and scattered to a stand of trees and nearby ravines. Sharpshooters made short work of them as they did, and Black Kettle and his wife fled with many others to seek safety across the river. A bullet struck Black Kettle in the back and another hit his wife; both fell from his horse into the icy water, where their bodies were recovered some time later.

When it was all over, Custer reported 103 warriors killed, yet by most accounts the large majority of those who died were old men, women, and children. The controversy did not end there. Custer, aware that there were likely more Indians in the vicinity, knew that he had to leave the area promptly. To deny the hostiles the use of the large Cheyenne pony herd, he ordered his men to kill over 800 of the animals. At first they tried cutting the throats, but when this proved inefficient, they resorted to guns. Many of the Cheyennes' provisions and belongings were also burned.

By now Custer could see more and more mounted warriors from downriver appearing in the distance, threatening to surround his position. As darkness began to fall, he determined to make a show of force as a way to buy time for his withdrawal back to Camp Supply. He assembled his men (and fifty-three women and children captives) into marching formation, and with the band playing, he moved in the direction of the villages downstream. The gambit was successful: the warriors were drawn away. The Seventh was able to reverse their direction under the cover of night, retracing their steps back to Black Kettle's ruined village and beyond.

The Seventh's own losses from the engagement were not inconsiderable. Only four were killed as a result of the fighting in the village, but another seventeen troopers under Major Joel Elliott died when he led them in pursuit of several Cheyenne trying to escape. They had gone too far out toward the gathering numbers of downriver warriors and were decimated. Custer was decidedly uncurious about their whereabouts—something that his men later held against him—and afterward merely listed them as "missing." He and his entire regiment might have met the same end, if Black Kettle had had an extra day to move his village closer to his allies. History might have preempted, rather than repeated, itself. Instead, at Little Bighorn in 1876, aware only that there was an unknown number of hostiles encamped along a shallow river ahead of him, Custer attempted to replay his exploits on the Washita. He divided his command . . . and charged.

Among the thousands there that overwhelmed him were some Cheyennes who had endured his campaign in Oklahoma. It is said that after the Battle of the Washita, a Cheyenne chief named Medicine Arrow had placed a curse on Custer: if he ever again made war upon the Cheyennes, he and the men of the Seventh would meet their doom.

INDOMITABLE

- 1873 -

Bitter Creek

ON NOVEMBER 5, 1873, A LARGE BODY OF KICKAPOO INDIANS arrived at their new reservation in northern Indian Territory, situated along the aptly named Bitter Creek. The Kickapoos were mostly women and children who earlier in the year had been forced from their homes on the Rio Grande and brought to Fort Gibson as "prisoners of war," though a better term might have been "hostages." The army hoped to use their captives as leverage to persuade several hundred other Kickapoos in Mexico to cease their cross-border raiding and return peaceably to settle once again in the United States.

To a considerable extent, the plan worked. More than 300 so-called Mexican Kickapoos, many of them warriors, agreed to come back to the Indian Territory and live on a reservation with their kidnapped kin. Most of them had been conveniently away on May 18, when Colonel R. S. Mackenzie and the Fourth Cavalry staged a carefully timed attack on the Rio Grande Kickapoo villages, invading

Mexico to do so. He wished to avoid full-scale battle with the warriors at all costs, and once the women, children, and old men were in
his hands—tied together two or three to a horse—he whisked them
away to the east and north as quickly as possible.

There was just one problem with the new reservation at Bitter
Creek: the returning warriors refused to accept it. They demanded to
select their own reservation in the Territory, which was promised as a
condition of their return. Amazingly, the government—which didn't
often keep its promises to Indians—agreed. There were still other
Kickapoos south of the border in Mexico, and anything that might
mollify the tribe was worth trying, if there was to be any chance of
bringing the rest back. The Kickapoo chiefs chose a tract of land near
the Shawnees and the Sacs and Foxes, not far from former lands
where some had settled years ago when allied with the Creeks.

Who were these people that the army was reluctant to fight and
the government was eager to please? "Intelligent, active, and brave,"
one observer had reported of the Kickapoos, they were always ready
to do battle, "provided that the odds are not more than six to one
against them." Their very presence in Mexico indicated their uncom-
promising, staunchly conservative stance: no schools, government
rations, or missionaries for them. They would stay true to the old
ways and go where they pleased. A small tribe originally from the
Great Lakes region, the Kickapoos already had a history—and
renown—in the Indian Territory and beyond when the Mackenzie
Raid at long last inaugurated the reservation era for them.

The Choctaws and Chickasaws certainly had tales to tell of the
Kickapoos. During the 1830s and 1840s, soon after those eastern
tribes were removed to their new lands in the Territory, their live-
stock, slaves, and other property were frequently stolen by bands of
Kickapoos ranging up and down the Washita Valley. When the
Choctaws and Chickasaws in joint council announced that they were

going to raise a militia to deal with the menace, the Kickapoos replied that they would relish the chance to "whip" such an army. Thoroughly intimidated, the Choctaws and Chickasaws never produced any troops, despite the fact that they outnumbered the Kickapoos by as much as twenty to one. "The Kickapoos have the highest reputation for courage and independence," E. A. Hitchcock noted during his travels in the Territory in 1842, "and I heard the opinion in the Choctaw nation, that the whole power of the nation could not subdue the Kickapoos in case of conflict." Finally the government intervened, establishing Fort Arbuckle and Fort Washita for the purpose of keeping the Kickapoos and other raiders in check. They continued their raids nevertheless.

Government officials were relieved somewhat in 1841, when the Creeks invited a large band of Kickapoos to live in the westernmost part of their lands. The Creeks recognized the Kickapoos' value as a buffer between them and the feared Comanches and Pawnees to the west. The Kickapoos were one of the few peoples whom the powerful Comanches respected, and they did a brisk business together in horses, cattle, whiskey, and captives. The Pawnees tried their best to get past the patrols that the Kickapoos mounted along the Creek Nation's borders, and the story was told of one unlucky group that in 1845 stole horses from some Kickapoo hunters, killing one man in the process. The Kickapoos went after the Pawnees seeking revenge, and they not only recovered their horses, but also killed one Pawnee and wounded several more. As a symbolic warning, the Kickapoos severed the dead Pawnee's arm and devoured the flesh from elbow to wrist.

The Kickapoos had one particular quality that made them good future Oklahomans: they did not like Texas, to put it mildly. In fact, they considered themselves to be at war with the Lone Star State virtually from its inception. From the north, crossing the Red River, and from the south, crossing the Rio Grande, the Kickapoos attacked and plundered Texas settlers relentlessly up to the time of the Mackenzie Raid in 1873. Their depredations were so severe by the early 1870s that, according to historian A. M. Gibson, they effectively rolled Texas counties back from the boundary with Mexico, so stripped of people and property had those areas become.

Probably the peak of Kickapoo animosity toward Texans occurred near the end of the Civil War, at a place called Dove Creek. The Kickapoos had been invited by the Mexican government to resettle in one of their northern states, and a large body of Kickapoos (including women and children) had left Indian Territory and was crossing west Texas peacefully, hoping simply to reach their destination. But their trail was spotted by Texas Confederate scouts, and on the cold morning of January 8, 1865, over 400 Confederate troops charged into the Kickapoo camp. The Kickapoos were startled at first, but they regrouped and drove the Texans into full retreat with devastating rifle fire. The Texans' casualties were twenty-six killed and more than sixty wounded—their worst defeat ever in the Indian wars—while the Kickapoos lost fifteen of their own. They continued on their way to Mexico.

It was in the aftermath of these long years of fierce warfare that the plan for the Mackenzie Raid was hatched—it was more subtle (and underhanded) than a direct assault. Thus the year 1873 was a momentous one for the Kickapoo people, as it signaled the end of nearly a century of hard-won independence from the United States. Yet the Kickapoos were not so easily cowed, as the government well knew. Many of them had abandoned a reservation in Kansas as recently as 1862. There were no guarantees that the Kickapoos might not do the same again, or continue their raiding parties. At their new Indian Territory reservation, Kickapoo chiefs played on these worries and procured extra supplies and annuities from officials during the 1870s and 1880s. When white settlers began to press for their reservation land, the Kickapoos held out until 1895, when the last land run in territorial history ended their reservation era. By then, many of the Kickapoos were making trips back and forth to Mexico to visit relatives, and eventually substantial numbers chose to remain south of the border, where they might live according to their own ways in peace.

BOOMER SOONER

- 1890 -

Oklahoma City

IT IS SOMEHOW APPROPRIATE THAT THE FIRST MAYOR OF Oklahoma City was killed in a dispute over land. In some sense he brought it on himself. William L. Couch had been a leader of the Boomer movement, which for years had agitated to open the lands of the Indian Territory to settlement. By the time President Harrison finally approved an opening in 1889, the Boomers' promotions had brought land hunger to a feverish pitch. There were far more claimants than there were good claims to go around, and fights became inevitable. As the fatal bullet crashed through his kneecap, the irony was probably lost on Couch.

The Boomers had actually been a rather peaceable lot. Since 1879, first under David L. Payne and later under Couch, they had pursued a kind of civil disobedience in the Territory. By the dozens and sometimes by the hundreds, they would go where they were forbidden and begin building cabins, clearing trees, and busting sod.

Then soldiers of the U.S. Army would appear, round them up, and escort them to the Kansas border. Couch had personally led six of these invasions. The Boomers never expected to stay. Instead, they sought to establish a principle—one that hardly needed to be established, that this was a "white man's country"—and to raise consciousness. They held meetings, published a newspaper, and mailed out flyers, promoting Oklahoma across the nation as a new Promised Land.

A later generation might call what the Boomers did "hype," but their hype worked only too well. On April 22, 1889, as many as 50,000 people crowded up to the borders of the Unassigned Lands, north, south, east, and west. There were approximately four home-seekers for each available plot. It truly was a race for land. Of course, some people hoped to improve on the odds, especially those like Couch and the Boomers who felt some sense of entitlement. Some flagrantly staked their claims well ahead of the big day, while others took jobs with the Santa Fe Railroad in order to be at a convenient location when the starting-guns went off. Still others, depending on their means and connections, also found a way into the territory before noontime. There were reports of some suspiciously well-coiffed "deputy marshals" hovering near town sites. Most "sooners," however, just lay in the weeds, awaiting the signal.

Oklahoma City was not entirely a blank slate when noon struck on its day of destiny, but it was close. Then known as Oklahoma Station, it featured only a railroad depot and a scattering of shacks, tents, and pens. When the great moment came, an eyewitness at the station, perched atop a boxcar, recalled that people seemed to materialize out of nowhere, scurrying in all directions, dragging luggage and tools. Within twenty minutes after twelve o'clock, at least forty new tents had been raised in the immediate vicinity. At about a quarter past one, the first apparently legitimate claim seekers arrived on the scene, looking around agape, their horses puffing.

Couch and various members of his family were among those well-placed employees of the Santa Fe Railroad who strolled from the tracks over to their claims sometime near noon. Couch had previously picked his plot out just west of the depot itself, a full 160-acre homestead soon to become famous. As the day progressed, seven more individuals also claimed the same parcel as a farm homestead, while almost 600 others demanded it be divided into town lots, because of its proximity to the railroad depot. Couch and his rival farm claimants, who had each staked out their own portions of the quarter-section and begun building houses, warned off all such comers, declaring that the land was not part of Oklahoma City. But in time the town lot-seekers became insistent enough that for several months army soldiers were stationed on the disputed property to keep the peace. The lot-seekers organized themselves and, Boomer-like, invaded the homestead repeatedly, trying to establish a foothold. Again, the irony of the situation was probably wasted on Couch.

Couch had bigger concerns—namely his immediate neighbors who had carved up the land he had so carefully chosen. Couch had resigned as mayor of Oklahoma City after only six months in order to "prove-up" his residence on the homestead, as required by law. He, his wife, and their five children lived in a small house on the property and put in a wheat field. They remained at a standoff with most of their fellow claimants, but from the beginning their relations were hostile with a man named John C. Adams. Among other incidents, Adams had chased one of Couch's sons off of his tract with a club, and on another occasion he shot and killed the family dog. Matters reached a crisis on April 4, 1890, when Adams chopped down part of a fence that Couch had constructed to keep Adams' horses out of his wheat. When Couch and one of his sons attempted to repair the fence, Adams came after them with a club, which Couch jerked away from him. Adams pulled out a revolver, but Couch drew his weapon faster, telling Adams to drop it. Couch's son picked up the gun, and he and his father retreated toward their house. Adams, meanwhile, had gone into his own home and emerged with a rifle. Shots were exchanged, and Couch was hit in the left knee.

The wound became infected, and Couch died two weeks later. Adams stood trial for murder and was sentenced to seven years in prison. There was a final irony that was most certainly lost on Couch: his funeral occurred on the first anniversary of the land run.

The dispute over the homestead next turned to legal channels. Of the seven rivals, the claims of the late Couch and several others were disallowed by the General Land Office because they were shown to be "sooners." The battle now boiled down to two individuals, John Dawson and Robert Higgins, a doctor from Kansas. Dawson strove to show that Higgins was also guilty of "soonerism," because he had crossed the starting line on April 22, 1889, to water his horses. Higgins contended that he had done so, but that he had witnesses to show that he had returned to his place and run the race legitimately. The case took five years to settle and went all the way up to the U.S. secretary of the interior, who decided in Dr. Higgins' favor.

Higgins gave the widow Couch twenty-one lots from the land her husband had once claimed. Most of the thousands of legal disputes that erupted out of the 1889 Land Run did not end so magnanimously. The opening of the lands had been symbolic of the frontier myth that Americans so fervently believed in, and when the Promised Land failed to be delivered to them, they did something that was also quintessentially American—they called on their lawyers.

DEAD OR ALIVE, PREFERABLY DEAD

- 1892 -

Rabbit Trap

FOR SOMEONE WHO WAS NEVER ACTUALLY CONVICTED of a crime, Ned Christie attracted a lot of attention from law enforcement. But to try him they first had to capture him, and there was the hitch. They found him easily enough; it was apprehending him that proved to be the hard part.

Ned Christie was an imposing six-foot four-inch Cherokee in his early forties who spoke broken English and by most accounts was an expert marksman and gunsmith. He was elected a Cherokee senator in 1885 and favored tribal sovereignty. Some scholars describe his five-year standoff with federal marshals as more of a rebellion than a manhunt. He was originally implicated in the murder of a deputy marshal named Dan Maples in 1887, based on the testimony of an alleged accomplice. There remains enough evidence to call into question Christie's role in the Maples murder and subsequent crimes laid at his feet. There is, however, no doubt that Christie was guilty of numerous counts of "assaulting an officer," as he turned away posse after posse sent to arrest him. From Christie's perspective, these were instances of self-defense. He had reason to be skeptical of a fair hearing in the infamous "Hanging Judge" Parker's courtroom at Fort Smith, especially as the years wore on and it became a matter of honor for the marshals of the district to bring him to justice.

Christie's closest call prior to his final reckoning came at the hands of an equally determined lawman, Deputy Marshal Heck Thomas. This encounter set the stage for what was to later happen in November of 1892.

In 1889 Thomas had departed from Vinita with three other deputies. They traveled south toward Rabbit Trap, the known location of Christie's cabin, and stealthily moved into position; Christie was often aided and warned ahead of time by family members or neighbors. Just before dawn, Thomas called out for Christie to surrender, or at least to send his wife out to safety. Christie instead began firing. In response the lawmen set his nearby gun shop ablaze, trying to flush Christie from his cabin, which also began to burn. Christie was able to hit one of the marshals while his wife ran for cover, but Christie's son, also attempting to run away, was seriously wounded when the lawmen mistook him for his father. Finally Christie himself broke for it, and Thomas shot him in the face, blinding him in one of his eyes. Nevertheless, he managed to escape deep into the woods, where friends found him and helped him to a doctor.

After a long period of hiding and recuperating, Christie returned to the vicinity of his destroyed home at Rabbit Trap and built a new structure on a more defensible site. This building, with its double-thick log walls reinforced by oak two-by-fours on a sandstone foundation, has come to be called "Ned's Fort"; Christie also provisioned it with plenty of food, water, and ammunition.

At least three earlier concerted attempts were made by marshals to storm the fort before the final showdown in 1892. The first happened in 1890 and is attributed to Bass Reeves, one of the few African American federal marshals. The fort was apparently damaged by fire, but Christie still succeeded in evading capture. The next two attacks were organized by Deputy Marshal Dave Rusk, who gathered large posses of Cherokees unfriendly to Christie in hopes of ending the stalemate. On his first try in 1891, Rusk saw four of his posse members wounded as soon as Christie began firing; he withdrew his men abruptly. Apparently, Christie also had a keen eye for Rusk's black hat and put more than one bullet through it. Rusk's second attempt was mustered in October of 1892, and although several outside buildings were set on fire, a flaming wagon pushed toward the fort, and dynamite employed (the fuse failed to light), this assault, too, was broken off after two deputy marshals were seriously wounded.

Finally the lot fell to Gus York and Gideon S. "Cap" White, who decided to try a different tactic. They ordered a small-bore cannon from an army post in Kansas, along with bullet-shaped shells that might pierce the thick walls of Ned's Fort. On the morning of November 3, 1892, York, White, and their large posse approached the site and surrounded Christie and his household. The engagement began with the usual calls for surrender; Christie did allow the women and children within the fort to leave. But remaining inside were Christie and three companions; their gunfire kept the lawmen at bay for several hours. Pinned down, the posse returned fire with gusto—as many as 2,000 rounds—but with little effect. Next the marshals tried shooting flaming arrows into the fort, yet these also proved useless.

At last the cannon arrived on the scene. The lawmen maneuvered it into position, blasting round after round into the walls and roof.

Surprisingly, the small shells produced little damage, punching only a few holes here and there. Doubling the powder charge, they tried again, but the cannon barrel blew up. Now without their secret weapon, the marshals decided to fortify a small wagon into a kind of rolling shield or barricade. As their comrades covered them with a furious burst of gunfire, two marshals were able to push close enough to the fort to set a large bundle of dynamite against one wall, trailing a long fuse. At daybreak the fuse was lit, and the explosion demolished the whole side of the fort, leaving the rest on fire.

Still Ned Christie did not surrender. He and his wounded friends retreated to the root cellar of the burning building, keeping up their gunfire at the posse. But as the fort began to collapse around them, Christie and the others had to run for it. Out in the open, Christie shot his Winchester at a group of deputies as he attempted to get past them; he was so close that he left a powder burn on the face of one of the men. The lawmen returned fire, and Christie fell dead. It is reported that the son of Dan Maples, whom Christie was alleged to have murdered several years before, then emptied his revolver into Christie's body.

Christie's remains were mounted on the door of the fort and carried back to Fort Smith, where Judge Parker no doubt viewed them with satisfaction and relief. The remains were displayed publicly for most of a Sunday before being returned to Christie's family via Fort Gibson. They buried him in a family cemetery in the Going Snake District, according to the manner of the Cherokees.

The members of the posse divided the $1,000 reward for Ned Christie, dead or alive. After expenses, it came to $74.00 per man.

TAKING BILL DOOLIN, TWICE

- 1896 -

Guthrie

WHEN DEPUTY MARSHAL BILL TILGHMAN FINALLY MADE an arrest of outlaw gang-leader Bill Doolin, it was like a scene from a Hollywood movie—but not the shoot 'em up variety. To be sure, neither man had ever been shy about using a gun. Yet when Tilghman saw that he might be able to take Doolin alive, he jumped at the chance. Unfortunately, Doolin would not let matters rest there.

The outlaw and lawman came face-to-face in a bathhouse at Eureka Springs, Arkansas, on December 5, 1895. Tilghman had arrived on a morning train after receiving word that a man fitting Doolin's description was staying at the resort, just across the border from Indian Territory. He entered a bathhouse intent on taking a soak himself, when suddenly he saw Doolin in an adjoining room, lounging on a couch, reading a newspaper. Reportedly, the two men exchanged looks and, after a pause, Doolin went back to his paper. Keeping a large stove between them, Tilghman strode into a nearby dressing room, drew his forty-five, and stepped out again to announce to Doolin that he was under arrest.

Doolin was startled and leapt up, trying to reach a pistol strapped underneath his vest. Tilghman held onto Doolin's coat sleeve, preventing him from unbuttoning. He called for the attendant to undo the vest and disarm Doolin, but in the midst of the operation, the attendant lost his nerve and fled with the gun at arm's length. Doolin still seemed inclined to struggle, and Tilghman reiterated that he wanted to bring him in alive. He had his forty-five now at point-blank range. After hesitating, Doolin surrendered. Tilghman put him in shackles and led him outside.

Tilghman had more reasons than extra reward money for capturing Doolin alive. According to several accounts, he believed that Doolin might have intervened once to save his life. In January of the same year, Tilghman and a colleague had been tracking Doolin's gang when they stopped one evening at the Dunn Ranch near Pawnee. Tilghman tried speaking to the rancher as to Doolin's whereabouts, but Dunn was downright rude in his response—purposefully so, as it turned out. Along the walls of the ranch house were multiple bunks with curtains drawn; Tilghman could hear men breathing behind them. After getting little information from Dunn, he left shortly, but with the realization that the gang itself or some other bunch of outlaws was hiding in the house. Tilghman went for reinforcements and was later informed by the rancher that Doolin, Bill Dalton, and several other gang members were in fact in those bunks at the time of Tilghman's visit, guns ready. Doolin prevented one of his gang members, a bloodthirsty man named Red Buck, from shooting Tilghman down that night, knowing that things would get hot for all of them if they dared to kill the well-known marshal.

As Tilghman and Doolin were leaving Eureka Springs for the trip back to Oklahoma Territory, Tilghman offered to remove Doolin's shackles on his honor not to escape. Doolin gave his word and kept it for the duration of the journey. He could only have been chagrined and downcast by the turn of events. He must have expected a bit more spectacular effort to catch him than one lone lawman preparing to take a bath. Two years earlier, at Ingalls, two dozen deputy marshals and posse members had attacked the Doolin's gang while they were recreating in the hotel and saloon of the small town; three deputies died, as did two townspeople, while one gang member was wounded and another captured. Doolin and his men had continued their crime spree since then, yet at the time of his surrender in Eureka Springs, there were rumors that Doolin was retiring. On April 3, 1895, his gang had robbed a train south of Dover that was carrying a $50,000 army payroll to Texas. It was their largest haul yet, and Doolin had a young wife and a toddler son whom he doted on. He was supposedly in Eureka Springs trying to recover his health, soothing the aches of some old gunshot wounds.

When Tilghman and his captive Doolin arrived in Guthrie, the territorial capital, 2,000 people were said to be waiting for a glimpse of the celebrated outlaw. Heck Thomas and several other deputy marshals escorted the pair to the marshal's office, where many citizens stopped by to meet Doolin and congratulate Tilghman. That evening Doolin was treated to dinner in a fine hotel before returning to bed in his jail cell.

Apparently, Bill Doolin was not feeling quite as generous as his hosts. In late June 1896, when fellow gang member "Dynamite Dick" Clifton was brought to the Guthrie jail, Doolin began scheming to escape. He faked an illness in order to have his cell changed and to gain access to a less restricted area called the bull pen. On the night of July 5, several inmates in the bull pen jumped a guard, who had carelessly left his gun unattended. Doolin grabbed this revolver and forced the guard to unlock several cells, including Dynamite

Dick's. Eight other men besides Doolin and Clifton escaped during the jailbreak.

If Doolin had accepted his fate after Eureka Springs, history might have recorded that elegant postscript to his career: two respected adversaries, on opposite sides of the law, facing off until one yielded peacefully. But the truth about outlaws like Bill Doolin was usually more brutal than elegant, and his career was destined to have a different ending.

Heck Thomas, one of the legendary "Three Guardsmen" of Oklahoma—along with Bill Tilghman and Chris Madsen—was to play the leading part in Doolin's final reckoning. Word reached Thomas in late August 1896 that Doolin had been spotted in the vicinity of his father-in-law's store near Lawson. Preparations seemed to be underway for a long trip somewhere. Thomas gathered a posse, and on the night of August 24, they set up an ambush nearby to net Doolin. Doolin, however, seemed to have been warned that neighborhood boys were spying on him; he appeared to be on edge as he led his horse down a moonlit lane close to midnight. He carried a Winchester. As he neared the posse's position, Thomas called out for him to put up his hands, as did another deputy across the road. Doolin whirled and fired off a shot close to Thomas, then drew a revolver and was about to fire again when Thomas let loose with a long-barreled shotgun. Doolin fell dead, his heart full of buckshot.

The same citizens who had earlier feted Bill Doolin now rejoiced that the country was rid of a dangerous man.

GALA DAY

- 1905 -

101 Ranch

Sitting on the seat of a brand new Locomobile, Geronimo raised his rifle and took aim at the buffalo. He fired, but the old bull wouldn't go down. He shot again and yet again, and finally the animal slumped to the ground. Geronimo was given a knife and joined in the butchering. Later, wearing a top hat, he sat behind the wheel of the Locomobile and posed for pictures. A thousand dollars had been offered to anyone allowing Geronimo to scalp them, but there were no takers.

This strange scene was like something out of a movie, and in a way, it was. June 11, 1905 was "Oklahoma's Gala Day" at the 101 Ranch, and the captive Geronimo was one of the star attractions, courtesy of the U.S. Army. The Gala Day event was the first large-scale public entertainment staged by the Miller brothers, proprietors of the ranch. Within a few years western movies would be filmed there, and the Millers would winter their traveling show near Hollywood, where 101 performers found ample work as extras. A number of performers eventually went on to major movie careers of their own, including Tom Mix, Hoot Gibson, and Buck Jones. They were already well versed in the Old West as show business, thanks to the Miller brothers.

The 101 Ranch empire was founded in 1879 by Colonel George Washington Miller, the brothers' father. The original leases totaled about 60,000 acres in the Cherokee Strip, and the 101 Ranch proper (established in 1893) grew over time to encompass nearly 110,000 acres. The colonel always did things on a grand scale, and as an agricultural operation, the 101 included not only thousands of cattle but also vast fields of wheat, corn, and cotton, as well as huge vegetable gardens and orchards. The ranch was so large that it had its own churches, schools, roads, and mail delivery.

All of those animals and crops—overseen from the ranch's famous White House headquarters—required the Millers to hire many hands and employees. And it was from among these ranch hands that the nucleus of a Wild West show was born. Like every ranch, the 101 needed its round-ups, and round-ups on such a scale became spectacles in and of themselves. In fact, the Miller family could make a claim to holding the world's first commercial rodeo— while on the Chisholm Trail in Kansas in 1882—and Bill Pickett, the African American rodeo star who invented steer wrestling, was a longtime performer in the 101 show. The Millers had been inviting friends and neighbors to watch their annual round-up for years prior to 1905. The place was already a tourist attraction. Thus when they were approached about providing some entertainment for the convention of the National Editorial Association to be held at Guthrie, they did not disappoint.

The Miller brothers had witnessed similar spectacles at the St. Louis World's Fair the previous year, and they had even accompanied a Wild West show to New York earlier in 1905, where they watched their friend Will Rogers get his first big break. The Millers therefore had plenty of ideas about how to stage the Gala Day event successfully. One way to attract attention was to take advantage of Oklahoma's large Native American population, which the Millers did, promising a colorful and exotic tableau to the eastern newspaper editors and others in the audience. Another means was copious publicity, free whenever possible—and so was launched the "scalped by Geronimo" dare, almost certainly a stunt. Still another story that brought exposure to the coming event was the rumor that the Millers were planning to present a buffalo hunt and kill off the ranch's small herd—this at a time when conservationists were fighting to save the last few remaining bison in the country. (Geronimo's tough old bull was actually the only one that died for viewing pleasure.) President Roosevelt reportedly became so alarmed by the prospect that he asked the territorial governor to dispatch troops to prevent any harm to the herd.

When June 11 arrived, train after train pulled into the railroad station of the small nearby town of Bliss, where tracks had been laid and switchmen brought in especially to accommodate the crowds. The trains were filled beyond capacity, with some people even riding on the roofs of the cars. Other visitors came by wagon or horse, until an estimated 65,000 people converged on the outdoor arena, generally considered to be the largest single assemblage ever seen in Oklahoma up to that date.

After the crowd feasted on soft drinks and ice cream, the show began at two o'clock with a mile-long parade led by the Miller brothers. Geronimo took his bows near the head of the line. Cavalry soldiers, numerous cowboys, hundreds of Indians, a wagon train, and thirteen marching bands made up the rest of the procession. Then followed the mock buffalo hunt performed by the Indians. Poncas, Pawnees, Osages, and members of other tribes swirled on their horses around dozens of bison in what was supposed to be quite a thrilling sight, even without bloodshed. After the Indians presented a ball-game, a powwow, and a war dance, trick-riders, bronc-busters, and other rodeo performers (including Pickett) took their turn in the arena. Another highlight of the event was the appearance of Lucille Mulhall, a young woman whose prowess at roping and riding was decidedly unladylike.

The grand finale occurred near sunset, when a line of covered wagons approached the arena and formed into a circle. People exited the wagons and began building fires and setting up camp, so that anyone who noticed would think they were latecomers to the show. Just then, hundreds of mounted Indians swooped down on them, firing their guns and letting loose their war cries. Soon some of the wagons were ablaze. Help arrived suddenly, as a swarm of cowboys descended on the Indians and drove them off. The crowd roared. It was melo-drama such that a thousand movie scenes would be made of.

Spurred by the success of Oklahoma's Gala Day, the Miller brothers staged a still larger show the following year to commemo-rate the opening of the Cherokee Strip. Over 500 cowboys and 1,000 Indians took part, watched by 50,000 spectators. In 1907, the Millers decided to take the 101 Ranch Wild West Show on the road, and it was a hit in the unlikely location of Norfolk, Virginia, at the Jamestown Exposition. In years to come, the show played to audi-ences throughout the United States, Canada, Mexico, and England, conveying the myth and spirit of the Old West well into the 1920s.

BUFFALO COMEBACK

- 1907 -

Wichita Mountains

In 1889, William T. Hornaday, a scientist at the Smithsonian Institution, estimated that there were 1,091 buffaloes left in the United States. He had been asked to mount a display of stuffed bison for the U.S. National Museum, but what he discovered in the process was that there were almost no buffalo left even for taxidermy. Sadder still, of those remaining 1,091, only 835 were wild animals—the rest lived mostly in zoos, farms, and ranches.

Hornaday's contemporaries believed that the number of bison that once roamed the Great Plains and other regions was as high as sixty million. The latest estimates now put the figure closer to thirty million, but in either case, the loss had been catastrophic, as Hornaday well realized. In the early 1900s, the word "conservation" was just beginning to be sounded on editorial pages, and it was usually applied to the problem of the nation's dwindling forests. Hornaday and others saw that there was also a need to preserve the last few majestic bison somewhere in their natural setting.

By 1905, the New York Zoological Park, where Hornaday had become director, had gathered a herd of forty-five bison from around the country, including ten calves born at the zoo. But where could they be sent that was both suitably wild and protected?

Luckily, the perfect natural venue already existed far to the west in the soon-to-be-born state of Oklahoma: the Wichita Mountains National Forest and Game Preserve. "Forest reserve" status was one means of protecting unique natural areas, and in this instance, it was President McKinley who had first set aside the Wichitas as a reserve in 1901 despite the fact that they did not exactly abound in trees. Later, President Theodore Roosevelt, who had personally hunted in the vicinity in the company of Comanche Chief Quanah Parker, was receptive to the idea of designating a portion of the Wichita reserve as a national preserve for buffalo. Roosevelt specifically urged Congress to do so in his 1905 annual message. The first wildlife preserve had been created at Pelican Island in Florida (1903), and with the support of groups such as the League of American Sportsmen, the Wichita Mountains reserve was to become the second such refuge in the country.

The concrete manifestation of the new refuge was seen in the form of a high fence that was to enclose about 8,000 acres of land carefully selected as habitat for bison. Congress appropriated $15,000 for the purpose, along with the construction of barns and corrals. An advance investigator for the New York Zoological Society, whose report helped to pass the bill in Congress, had noted that the area included plentiful grazing land and several good sources of water, as well as ravines and canyons that would provide shelter to the animals in winter.

Preparations for the arrival of the bison were ongoing in 1906 and 1907, and when all was ready, fifteen animals were selected from the Zoological Society's herd: six cows of breeding age, two younger cows, four young bulls, two calves (male and female), and one large older bull named "Comanche." This nucleus of a herd was chosen to represent four distinct bloodlines in order to prevent the effects of inbreeding. At least one of those bloodlines originated at the Goodnight Ranch in the Texas Panhandle, so some of these bison were very well-traveled when they arrived at their final destination!

On October 10, 1907, the animals were crated in New York and loaded onto stock cars, with shipping costs donated by the various railroads along the route. They left on October 11, drawing curious onlookers wherever they stopped between New York and Oklahoma. Finally, on October 17, the cars rolled into the small depot at Cache, greeted by a large throng who had converged to witness the historic occasion. Most accounts took particular notice of the Native Americans in the crowd, some of whom paid homage to the buffalo by wearing full tribal regalia. (It was no coincidence that the population of Native Americans in the United States also reached its historic low point at virtually the same time as the bison.) Quanah Parker was among the crowd. He had earlier expressed his strong support for a buffalo refuge with these words: "Tell the President that the buffalo is my old friend, and it would make my heart glad to see a herd once more roaming around Mount Scott."

The bison were unloaded from the train still in their crates. Comanche, the big bull, apparently had had enough of confinement; he proceeded to kick open the side of his crate. Frank Rush, the warden at the preserve who had accompanied the animals on their journey, was able to keep the surly bull contained, and the new herd was hauled in wagons the rest of the way to the refuge, where they were released.

The herd seemed to be taken from good stock. Within a month of their arrival, the first calf was born, and in honor of statehood day on November 16, 1907, Rush named the newborn "Oklahoma." One of the bull calves from the original herd grew to record size—almost 2,800 pounds. And over the years, the herd gradually increased in numbers, reaching 100 by 1918, 330 by 1938, and nearly 1,000 by the fiftieth anniversary of their introduction.

By the early 1970s, it was recognized that 1,000 bison was probably too many animals for the refuge to support, especially given the presence of several hundred longhorn cattle and elk on the same range. Overgrazing was becoming a problem, and so officials decided in 1971 to cut the size of the herd roughly in half. Thereafter the number fluctuated between 400 and 700 animals, the excess being sold off at a yearly auction.

As one of the prime attractions at the Wichita Mountains National Wildlife Refuge, the bison herd brought many thousands of tourists to the area annually, an influx that caused its own problems. Picnickers and hikers too often left garbage behind on their visits, and as many as ten buffaloes per year died from eating plastic bags or aluminum cans. At the same time, there were periodic reports of visitors being gored or trampled by a buffalo, resulting in serious injuries. Even in this protected place that was so much smaller than their former continental domain, the bison remained very much wild animals.

By the beginning of the twenty-first century, thanks to efforts at places like the Wichita Mountains refuge—several such "seed herds" had been established across the West—the population of bison nationwide approached a quarter of a million. Yet of that number, only a small percentage lived from year to year in a wild state, an existence such as they could still find at their home in Oklahoma's Wichita Mountains.

HOLD YOUR NOSE AND SIGN

- 1907 -

Guthrie

SOMETIMES WHEN VISITORS CAME TO HER HOME near Tishomingo, Mrs. William H. Murray would show them a set of rusty bedsprings in the backyard. On those springs, she would say proudly, the constitution of Oklahoma was written.

Alice Murray was biased, of course. No single man was responsible for the constitution, even if her husband, "Alfalfa Bill," had retired to his farm à la Thomas Jefferson to study the constitutions of ages past. Reclining thoughtfully in his overalls on the bedsprings, he had produced drafts of *something,* it is true. But the final constitution of Oklahoma—all 50,000 words of it, the longest in the world at the time—emerged out of the clash of numerous strong personalities, vested interests, crusading reformers, and, above all, partisan politics.

Certainly, Murray played his part. With four or five others in the Indian Territory, he had co-written the 35,000-word constitution for the proposed state of Sequoyah, which never materialized. Some full provisions from that stillborn document were eventually transcribed by Murray and his cohort onto the proposed constitution for Oklahoma. The Sequoyah warm-up also served Murray well in that he was elected president of Oklahoma's subsequent constitutional convention in 1906. He got himself unofficially on each of the drafting committees and did, in fact, write some parts of the ultimate constitution. He wanted nothing more in life than to be a founding father.

But there were two other important figures who influenced events leading to Oklahoma statehood, two titans of the national political scene: Republican president Theodore Roosevelt and perennial Democratic presidential candidate William Jennings Bryan. It was Roosevelt who did much to undermine any chance for a state of Sequoyah, when he made it known that he wanted Indian Territory and Oklahoma Territory to enter the union as a single state, not as separate ones. Roosevelt was never particularly enthusiastic about Oklahoma statehood on any terms, however; the state promised to be dominated by Democrats.

For exactly the same reason, Bryan—the "Boy Orator" from Nebraska—became a champion of Oklahoma statehood, and they loved him for it. Actually, they loved him anyway. In 1907, when he visited the Twin Territories during the weeks before the popular vote on the constitution, Bryan was greeted by throngs of people in a way that was surprising for someone who didn't hold public office. At Vinita, all of the town's schools and businesses closed; at McAlester, a parade more than a mile long, featuring brass bands and hundreds of miners with lamps glowing, was formed in his honor. Bryan shook so many hands that his own became swollen and sore. His speeches sounded a theme along these lines: Oklahoma has "the best Constitution of any state in this union and a better constitution than the Constitution of the United States."

President Roosevelt was of a different mind; his thoughts on the proposed constitution were "not fit to print." (Depending on the source, either Roosevelt or William Howard Taft may have referred to the framers as a "zoological garden of cranks.") Early in the drafting process, Roosevelt had already intervened to prevent Murray and other white supremacist Democrats from including one of their favorite planks, a provision to racially segregate train station waiting rooms and passenger cars. As for the rest of the document, Roosevelt dispatched Taft, his war secretary (who would defeat Bryan for the presidency the following year), to act as the official killjoy. "I would reject the constitution, I would vote it down," Taft told Oklahomans in August of 1907, "for it is no constitution at all."

What was wrong with it? First and foremost, according to Taft, "it goes into the utmost detail with respect to a great many things. It is complicated beyond any constitution I ever examined." Taft considered it less a true constitution than a 50,000-word "code of by-law." One such micromanaging provision that has since become infamous stated, "The flash test . . . for all kerosene oil for illuminating purposes shall be one hundred and fifteen degrees Fahrenheit." Taft complained that voters were having the constitution "shoved down [their] throats without . . . knowledge of what it means and what its effect shall be." Some of Taft's—and by extension, Roosevelt's—criticisms were well taken, while other comments revealed his own prejudices favoring wealth and big business. As Taft warned, the many articles in the constitution seeking to regulate corporations threatened to make them "slaves of the legislature." He asked, "Is that a square deal? I don't think it is."

Murray, Bryan, and the other supporters of the constitution did want a square deal—for ordinary people, as they saw it. Beyond seeking to constrain big corporations and monopolies, the proposed constitution embodied many of what were seen as the most progressive reforms of the day, including consumer protection against price gouging and impure food, graduation of taxes according to ability to pay, the eight-hour day for certain occupations, and prohibitions on child labor. To enhance democracy, the constitution also provided for the popular election of almost every state officer as well as the initiative and referendum at all levels of government. The framers enshrined all of these provisions and more into the constitution to prevent them from being easily overturned by future legislatures and special interests.

Oklahoma reformism did have its limits, though. Roosevelt may have temporarily thwarted Jim Crow railroad facilities from being written into the constitution, but racially segregated schools found their place in Article I, listed even before the Bill of Rights. Advocates hoping to secure women the right to vote were also turned away by Murray and other leaders of the constitutional convention.

Flaws and all, the constitution was overwhelmingly approved by voters on September 17, 1907. Roosevelt signaled that he would yield to this result—a close vote might have left him room to reject it. As Bryan crowed, "[T]he voice of the people has force in it and the president has wisely bowed to the demand for statehood so emphatically made by the people of Oklahoma." Yet two more months elapsed before Roosevelt could bring himself to sign a statehood proclamation. It happened on November 16, in a decidedly muted White House ceremony. At 10:16 A.M., using a quill pen, Roosevelt signed his name and said simply, "There, that makes Oklahoma a state." He looked up at a group of Republican officials who had gathered to witness, nodded his head, then left the room without another word. Reportedly, he did smile at one point.

Two minutes later, the news reached Oklahoma. In Guthrie, the capital, train whistles blew, bells rang, guns were fired, bands played, and people shouted and cheered in jubilation. But putting a slight damper on the celebration was the knowledge that within a few hours, every saloon in the state would close its doors—for decades. Besides ratifying the constitution, voters in September had also approved an amendment for a statewide prohibition on liquor. It was the first of 129 amendments to the constitution that were to be passed in the next eighty years of the state's history, in contrast to the twenty-seven amendments to the U.S. constitution over a 200-year period.

And so, a new state was born.

LAND OF THE REDS

- 1917 -

Seminole County

OKLAHOMANS LIKE TO THINK OF THEIR STATE AS CONSERVATIVE. Yet there was a time in the state's history, now mostly forgotten, when Oklahomans joined and voted for the Socialist Party in numbers higher than virtually anywhere else in the country. During the 1910s, dozens of Socialists were elected to local and state offices, and in many counties, Republicans were replaced by Socialists as the main competition for the ruling Democratic Party. How did this political oddity come to be?

The roots of socialism's popularity lay in the ruined hopes of people who had moved to Oklahoma expecting a Promised Land. The dream was to own a farm, and to live and work as one's own man, providing well for one's family. But on the very heels of the land runs of the 1890s, this dream began to prove elusive for increasing numbers of farmers across the Oklahoma countryside. Some found their property heavily mortgaged, while many others became renters or tenants. What the small farmers and the tenant farmers had in common was low crop prices and high debts. Tenants in particular had to pledge their crops against the debts that would see them through until harvest-time, and somehow there was never enough return to clear the books. It went on that way, year after year. They felt as if their lives were under the control of the landlords, bankers, cotton-gin owners, storekeepers, and other powers-that-be of the farm economy. By 1915, over half of all farmers statewide were tenants, and in the counties where the Socialists were to be the strongest, the number was as high as 80 to 90 percent.

These hard realities did not sit well with farmers who had been raised on the ideals of Thomas Jefferson, who told them they were the "chosen people of the earth," and that the independent, landowning farmer was the pillar of democracy. And so they formed a receptive audience for politicians and political organizations that related to their condition and vowed to make things better. Many of the state's political leaders, especially among the Democrats, were big landlords themselves, and thus less than sympathetic to the plight of their tenants. Socialist leaders like Oscar Ameringer, on the other hand, spoke in a language that expressed the grievances of the rural poor. They depicted the landlords and bankers as "parasites" on the people who actually worked the land and proposed to abolish rent— a man should only own as much land as he could farm himself. They published newspapers, put on picnics, and held camp meetings that were like evangelical revivals; in fact, the party grew to include ministers from the Baptist, Methodist, and Pentecostal-Holiness churches. The brotherhood of man, the Golden Rule, the Sermon on the Mount, and the rich man's chances to enter the kingdom of heaven were just some of the teachings from the Bible that brought the message of socialism home to the traditionally religious people in the crowds, which sometimes numbered over 10,000. To the Socialists, these encampments were a very visible expression of "class solidarity," but to the poor farmers themselves, they signified hope.

Support for the Socialists was greatest in over two dozen southeastern and western Oklahoma counties, including Dewey, Marshall, Roger Mills, Seminole, Beckham, Johnston, and Love. In 1912, Socialist presidential candidate Eugene Debs received only 6 percent of the vote nationally, but he won over 25 percent of the vote in these counties, and over 16 percent statewide; two Socialist congressional candidates also polled over 20 percent of the vote in their districts. In 1914, Socialist gubernatorial candidate Fred Holt received 21 percent of the vote statewide, while another Socialist running for Congress scored 33 percent, only ten points below the winning Democrat. More than 175 state and local Socialist candidates won their elections in 1914, including six for the state legislature.

The Democrats felt the Socialists breathing down their necks, and for the 1916 elections, they began to take steps, both legal and illegal, to meet the threat. They passed a law that put Democratic registrars in place at the local level, which would allow them to hold down the Socialist turnout. When the Socialists apparently succeeded in passing a referendum that would give them a seat on election boards throughout the state, Democratic officials manipulated the rules so that the measure, which received 147,000 votes statewide and won by a 30,000-vote margin, was overturned.

Many Socialist Party members were frustrated by these developments, and some began to question whether they could make any headway toward their ultimate goal, the "cooperative commonwealth," through the political system. Then, in 1917, came U.S. involvement in World War I and the threat of the draft. Socialists throughout the country spoke out against the "rich man's war, poor man's fight," and in Oklahoma, they did more than talk. A splinter group of Socialist tenant farmers called the Working Class Union (WCU) had been active for several years in more direct forms of action, such as arson, blacklisting, boycotts, and night-riding. But the possibility of the draft inflamed its members and made them still more radical. The secret organization, which claimed to have 35,000 members in Oklahoma and Arkansas, may also have become involved in various acts of sabotage, including the dynamiting of a water tank at Dewar and the sewer mains at Henryetta.

Matters came to a head in late July and early August of 1917, in an event that has come to be known as the Green Corn Rebellion. Two antiwar agitators, H. H. Munson and Homer Spence, both out on bond after having been arrested for inciting against the draft, began to stir up protest in Seminole and nearby counties. Over the next few days, hundreds of like-minded, armed WCU members began to organize in scattered locations through the area. They vowed to march in force to Washington, D.C., gathering recruits to their cause along the way and living off green corn until they reached their destination. They planned to burn bridges, cut telephone lines, and cause general disruption, and when President Wilson at last saw how many were opposed to the draft, they hoped he would abandon the war effort.

The tenuous plan was a measure of their desperation. August 2 saw the first shots fired, when a group of black WCU members crossed paths with the local sheriff. On August 3, a posse over a thousand strong descended on the various WCU camps. Gunfire broke out, and in the end three were killed. Over 450 were arrested, and about one-third of these were convicted.

The quick end of the Green Corn Rebellion signaled the start of a wider and more fervent wartime government witch-hunt of Socialists and other radicals throughout Oklahoma. Many Socialist leaders and organizers, who were guilty only of opposing the war, were jailed and their newspapers censored. The Socialist Party in Oklahoma never recovered. The degree to which the repression crushed them as a viable alternative party was shown in the election results: in 1916, over 47,000 Socialists had cast votes in statewide races; in 1918, only 7,000 did so.

In the 1920s, with no political alternatives left to offer hope, Oklahoma's poor farmers began to vote with their feet. They moved to the cities or left the state altogether to find better opportunities elsewhere. It was the beginning of the flood tide of Okie migration that was in coming years to shrink the population of Oklahoma, no longer a Promised Land.

BURNING GREENWOOD

- 1921 -

Tulsa

SEVEN-YEAR-OLD RALPH ELLISON NEVER FORGOT WHAT he saw in the summer of 1921, when he and his family passed through the Greenwood section of Tulsa on their way home to Oklahoma City. Several months earlier, when they had stayed with relatives in Greenwood en route to Indiana to look for work, the black neighborhood had a bustling business district, fine homes and churches, and its own hotels and newspapers. Now all of that was obliterated, replaced by a wasteland of charred ground on which the former residents lived as refugees in tents. This scene from the Tulsa Race Riot remained with Ellison for the rest of his life, and even haunted the pages of his posthumous novel, *Juneteenth*.

African American settlers, including Ellison's own parents, had originally come to Oklahoma as a land of opportunity, where they hoped to prosper to a degree that they were unable to in the Old South. Caught up in the frontier spirit, they founded all-black towns like Boley and Taft, and they built vibrant neighborhoods like Green-wood and Oklahoma City's Deep Deuce, where the Ellisons lived. Yet the new state of Oklahoma proved to be less than welcoming to blacks, despite all of their enterprise. Public schools were segregated under the state constitution, and the first order of business for the new state legislature was to enact racial segregation in public accommodations. There were other means to enforce the color line as well—terror, for one. No less than twenty-three blacks (including two women) were lynched in Oklahoma during the decade before the Tulsa riot.

Although they were kept at the margins of society, black Tulsans had shared to an extent in the oil-based prosperity of the city. Tulsa's population grew from 10,000 in 1910 to over 100,000 in 1920. Such growth had its costs, exacerbated by the stresses and displacements of World War I, just recently concluded. Crime and vice were prevalent in parts of the city, while wartime intolerance persisted, directed against anyone whose color, background, or behavior failed to measure up to white Anglo-Saxon "100% Americanism." It was no accident that the vigilante Ku Klux Klan found a fertile recruiting ground in 1920s Oklahoma. At the same time, the ideas of black nationalist Marcus Garvey, preaching resistance and self-assertion, were circulating on the streets of Greenwood. African American veterans of the war, who had fought to make the world safe for democracy, wanted to see a little more of it at home.

The riot itself—some historians prefer to term it a "race war" or "ethnic cleansing"—occurred in the midst of this tense atmosphere. On May 31, a black teenager named Dick Rowland was arrested for the alleged assault of Sarah Page, a white elevator operator. The charges, already questionable, were later dismissed. Tulsa newspapers published inflammatory articles and editorials on the incident, and by late evening, a mob of more than 2,000 whites gathered at the county jail with lynching on their minds. From Greenwood, over a hundred black men arrived at the jail, rallying to Rowland's defense. There were guns carried on both sides, and the situation quickly got out of control. Shots rang out, and more than a dozen blacks and whites fell dead or wounded.

This 10:00 P.M. melee was merely the opening act of the Tulsa Race Riot, considered to be the worst in American history. The blacks retreated quickly to Greenwood to ready their defenses, while the enraged whites broke into hardware stores and pawnshops, procuring all manner of weapons, including a mounted machine-gun. At first, they roamed the downtown area, attacking any black person unlucky enough to be in the wrong place at the wrong time. One witness told of a mob chasing a black man down an alley and into a movie theater. The man ran onto the stage, blinded by the projector, and was felled by a shotgun blast.

Through the middle hours of the night, the two sides exchanged gunfire across a railroad yard separating Greenwood from white Tulsa. Some blacks wrongly concluded that they had held off the rampaging whites. But the rampage had not yet begun. As daylight approached, thousands of armed white men mobilized at the railroad yard, preparing to invade Greenwood. They put the machine-gun on a nearby grain elevator, and as it strafed the opposite tracks, the whites charged, shouting and yelling. Soon airplanes were overhead, shooting at fleeing blacks and, by some accounts, dropping explosives.

The white rioters swept through Greenwood methodically, ordering people from their homes, looting valuables, setting fire to the houses, and marching blacks to three different "internment" centers. Anyone who resisted was shot, as were many who did not. Dr. A. C. Jackson, a black surgeon and pillar of the community, was reportedly killed by a group of whites when he left his home with his hands up in surrender.

Pockets of black defenders held off the invading whites at locations across Greenwood. A number were posted in the belfry of the recently finished Mount Zion Baptist Church, acting as snipers to keep the rioters at bay. The whites brought in the machine-gun from the grain elevator and opened up on the belfry, silencing them. The church was put to the torch, as were several others in the neighborhood.

Throughout the madness of that day, Tulsa law enforcement did little to stop the carnage and in many ways abetted it. They had deputized numerous rioters, who literally took the law into their own hands. Police also participated in the arrest and confinement of blacks at the internment centers, ostensibly for their own protection. Tulsa National Guard units blatantly sided with the rioters rather than trying to disarm them.

National Guard troops from Oklahoma City belatedly arrived at mid-morning, and martial law was declared for the county close to noon. Order was gradually restored as more units came into the city from other parts of the state. The riot was pronounced over by 8:00 P.M. Virtually all of the surviving blacks in Tulsa—except for those who had escaped or were in hiding—were under arrest in the makeshift internment centers.

Over 1,200 homes in Greenwood were destroyed during the riot, as were the stores and offices of what had once been known as the "Black Wall Street." As the young Ralph Ellison saw, many were forced to spend the winter months living in tents provided by the Red Cross. Others were taken in by sympathetic white families in Tulsa, ashamed of what had happened in their city. The final death toll has remained uncertain, in part because of the completeness of the destruction. The confirmed number is thirty-nine (including twelve whites), though estimates of the number of blacks who died range from 150 to 300. There were reports of mass graves, as yet undiscovered.

Not surprisingly, a Tulsa grand jury blamed the riot on a "Negro uprising." No whites were ever punished for their role in the conflagration. Black victims found little success with insurance or legal claims, at the time or subsequently. In 1997, after many years of silence and neglect, the state legislature appointed a commission to study the riot. The commission recommended that reparations be paid to the survivors and descendants, that scholarships be established, that economic aid be given to Greenwood, and that a memorial be constructed. In 2001, legislators did pass the "1921 Tulsa Race Riot Reconciliation Act," but it omitted reparations. A class-action lawsuit brought on behalf of a number of elderly riot survivors went all the way to the U.S. Supreme Court, which in 2005 agreed with lower courts in ruling against the survivors and in favor of Tulsa and the state of Oklahoma. College scholarships and a memorial seemed the most likely outcome of years of advocacy and agitation. It would be the second such memorial constructed; the people of Greenwood had installed their own memorial in 1996. Thus did Tulsa and the state as a whole begin the long process of recognition and healing.

In 1926, five years after the riot, the renowned African American intellectual W.E.B. Du Bois visited Tulsa. Greenwood by then was well on its way to being rebuilt by its residents. Just as before, they did it with little outside help, through their own hard work and determination. Du Bois was impressed by what he saw. He understood now why no lynching had taken place in Tulsa on that day in 1921. Instead, he noted with admiration, there had been a war.

WILD MARY AND NO. 1 STOUT

- 1930 -

Oklahoma City

ON THE COLD, EARLY MORNING OF March 26, 1930, there was nothing to indicate that this oil well would be different from any of the dozens that had already been sunk in the Oklahoma City field. As the tired rig crew finished their work for the night, little did they know that the I.T.I.O.-Foster No. 1 Mary Sudik was about to become known around the world, the most famous Oklahoma oil well of them all.

This was the era when Oklahoma and oil were still synonymous. Commercial drilling dated back to 1897, when the Nellie Johnstone No. 1 was brought in at the Bartlesville-Dewey field, the first of a series of major strikes that would rank Oklahoma first nationally in oil production when it entered the union in 1907. The fabulous Glenn Pool was the most important of these early fields. Its quality and quantity led the oil industry to beat a path to Oklahoma's door, and companies like Gulf and Texaco constructed pipelines hundreds of miles long solely to tap its high-grade crude. Consequently, some great American fortunes owed much to the Glenn Pool field, including those of Harry Sinclair and the Mellon family. It also helped to make Tulsa, credibly, the "oil capital of the world."

As significant as the Glenn Pool field was to the development of Oklahoma's oil industry, it was eclipsed in total production by some subsequently discovered fields, such as the Cushing, the Burbank, and, in 1928, the Oklahoma City field. Over the next several decades, Oklahoma City would remain one of the top ten most productive fields in the country, yielding almost 800 million barrels of oil. But initially, as drillers were quick to find, getting the oil out of the ground was complicated by high natural gas pressure. When released, the gas drove the oil-laden sands thousands of feet upward out of the well shaft at high velocity, higher than a sandblaster. The sand could tear through seals and valves meant to control the flow from the well. When that happened, they had themselves a gusher.

There were ways of preventing gushers, but on the morning of March 26, after working a twelve-hour shift, the crew on the Mary Sudik rig got a little careless. They had reached the oil-sands at the 6,470-foot level and were removing the drill pipe to replace it with permanent pipe. But they neglected to keep the hole filled with "mud" while doing so, which would have contained the gas and oil far underneath. Instead, with a deafening roar, the gas rushed from the well, blowing twenty heavy lengths of pipe skyward with such force that they were bent and twisted when caught in the upper structure of the derrick. The ferocious stream of gas ran invisibly at first, but gradually it colored into a dark brownish gold, as the gushing mist of crude oil glinted in the sun. Occasionally, an oil rainbow could be seen.

"Wild Mary," as the well came to be known, was not the first gusher in the Oklahoma City field, or the last, or even the biggest.

But there was something about it that captured the world's imagination. The plume of the gusher, hundreds of feet high, was visible for miles, and depending on the wind direction, it coated trees, grass, and houses nearby. It speckled white shirts and windshields up to twelve miles away. Each day for eleven days, Wild Mary shot out 20,000 barrels of oil and 200 million cubic feet of gas. Pits, ditches, and gullies surrounding the well filled up with large ponds of oil. A two-square-mile evacuation zone was established around the area to prevent the possibility of fire. The smallest spark might cause a conflagration in much of the city.

Crews working to contain the well had to wear slicker suits, army helmets, and earplugs. On March 30, they made their first major attempt at capping the well, but the fix only held for twelve hours before the blast of sand from below ate away the equipment and caused it to fail. After several days of preparing more fittings, they tried again on April 4, using grab hooks to maneuver and fasten down a heavy cap known as an "overshot." The overshot whipped back and forth in the blast of the gusher as the men struggled to hold it steady. Suddenly, there was blessed silence. The morning headlines on the following day announced their success.

But within a few hours, the overshot failed and Wild Mary erupted again. The next day, a 3,000-pound device called a "die nipple" was screwed onto the casing of the well and miraculously, it held. Workers immediately set about skimming up the oil from where it had fallen nearby—over 200,000 barrels were recovered. In years to come, the Wild Mary Sudik went on to produce, much more quietly, another 800,000 barrels.

As if Wild Mary were not awesome enough, the world soon learned that the Oklahoma City field had yet one more spectacular show to put on in 1930. The Morgan Petroleum No. 1 C.E. Stout well, usually referred to as the "No. 1 Stout," broke loose and became a gusher on the day before Halloween. Officials knew the procedure by now and cordoned off a large area around the site. Several schools in the vicinity were closed, the Salvation Army took in displaced residents, and a watch was set to prevent fires.

Although it lasted only three days, the No. 1 Stout threw out an enormous amount of crude oil. Estimates ranged from 60,000 barrels per day up to 75,000. It was successfully capped on November 2, using many of the same methods that had worked on the Wild Mary. But the No. 1 Stout show was not over yet.

So much oil had accumulated into ponds behind earthen dykes that one of the dykes broke, spilling oil into the North Canadian River. Three inches thick in places, the oil spread for miles, killing fish and birds along the river. Then, on November 2, the river caught fire. Flames shot forty feet into the air and thick, black smoke rolled high into the sky, visible as far away as Enid. A strong enough current kept the flames from traveling upstream, back to the well area. Gradually the oil burned itself off. But on the next day, more fires flared up miles farther downstream, near the towns of Spencer, Harrah, and McLoud, destroying two bridges. These fires, too, dissipated, but for many years afterward people remembered the "river of fire" that had come from No. 1 Stout.

Nearly half a million oil wells in total have been drilled in Oklahoma over its entire history, producing over 14 billion barrels of oil. Yet out of all of those wells, none ever created quite as much spectacle as the two great gushers of 1930, Wild Mary Sudik and No. 1 Stout.

KING TUT'S TOMB, OKLAHOMA-STYLE

- 1933 -

Spiro

FOR YEARS ODD STORIES AND SUPERSTITIONS HAD circulated in the backwoods about the grassy mounds that lay on the Craig property outside of Spiro. Horses shied up when they were in the vicinity, and strange blue flames could be seen there at night. Stranger still, an earlier owner claimed once to have witnessed a tiny wagon emerge from the largest mound, pulled by a team of cats. There was the general opinion that the mounds were haunted and not a good place to be after dark.

Beyond the isolated farms along that stretch of the nearby Arkansas River, the mounds and their tales were little known. And no one, not even the neighbors, realized that the mounds comprised one of the most important archaeological sites in the United States. Obscurity had saved them—at least until 1935, when word of the treasures they contained began to spread around the world.

People had been finding relics in the area since anyone could remember. There had been a small amount of digging on the largest mound, known as Craig Mound, twenty years earlier, though little was uncovered. J. B. Thoburn of the Oklahoma Historical Society visited the mounds in 1913, but the owner refused to allow him to do any excavating. Thoburn took the earliest known photograph of the site, important for later researchers. He concluded correctly that the mounds were associated with the ancestors of contemporary Native Americans and were related to similar sites in Arkansas and elsewhere in the South.

After this brief period of interest, the mounds retreated into obscurity again until the summer of 1933, when a local man, R. W. Wall, convinced the owner of the property to sign a two-year lease (reportedly for $350) with a group of half a dozen men calling itself the Pocolo Mining Company. Although previous owners had been good stewards of the mounds, the current owner, a preacher named George Evans, may have found any offer hard to refuse in the depths of the Great Depression.

The Pocolo group went to work and showed that it was aptly named. Using the crudest and most destructive methods, the men sunk holes haphazardly into the mounds, throwing away shards of pottery, pieces of textiles, and other evidence that might have been invaluable to scientists. When the yields of artifacts were not satisfying enough, they then resorted to tunneling, hiring local coal miners for extra help. The largest of the tunnels, through Craig Mound, was big enough for a man with a wheelbarrow. By now some of the wonders of the mounds were being revealed—finely carved maces and pipes, ornately engraved shells, beautiful masks, beads, pearls, along with, of course, human remains. Near the center of the Craig Mound, which soon came to be known as the "Great Temple Mound," the Pocolo men claimed to have discovered an inner chamber, buttressed by cedar poles, enclosing a skeleton in ceremonial garb. They used the cedar poles for firewood, another great loss to science—not to mention the fact that they were clearly robbing a grave.

As the Pocolo partnership began to market its finds to dealers nationally, word spread through professional archaeology circles and made its way to F. E. Clements, head of the anthropology department at the University of Oklahoma. Clements and other investigators undertook trips to observe the operations at the site and were appalled by what they saw. Newspaper reporters also arrived on the scene, including one from Kansas City who likened the discovery to King Tut's tomb, a worldwide sensation when it was found a decade or so earlier. Prices and demand for the artifacts skyrocketed with all of the publicity, and Clements realized that something had to be done to preserve Spiro and similar sites from further looting.

Thanks to public pressure, the Oklahoma legislature passed a law in the spring of 1935 to protect the state's antiquities, requiring interested parties to apply for permission to excavate through the OU Department of Anthropology. The penalty for violators was a $200 fine or thirty days in jail. The Pocolo company ignored the new law and continued with their digging until they received a warning from the local sheriff's office. They packed up and left, but only temporarily. At this point Professor Clements, with very bad timing, accepted a summer teaching job in California and thus left the Spiro site unmonitored. The Pocolo partners returned and did some of their dirtiest work in his absence, which included dynamiting part of the Craig Mound. Finally their lease ended in November 1935, and they were done.

Meanwhile, the fame of the site only grew. The Tut analogy appeared to be coming true: the place seemed to have a curse associated with it. R. W. Wall, who had negotiated the Pocolo lease, fell in a creek nearby and drowned under suspicious circumstances. One of the two heirs to the property, a sixteen-year-old boy, died of tuber-culosis during the controversy while living at the site. And a local attorney who opposed the new antiquities law also died by strange coincidence. Such stories only served to drive the price of Spiro arti-facts even higher, and to start a bidding war among dealers for what was left of the mounds.

Clements and state officials realized that further steps had to be taken to secure the site for the public interest. The state acquired a lease and teams of excavators, overseen by the universities of Oklahoma and Tulsa. Excavators spent several years (1936-41) salvaging scientific information from the mounds. As it turned out, many of the artifacts sold by the Pocolo vandals were eventually acquired by respected insti-tutions, including a large collection at the Peabody Museum of Har-vard University. An archaeological park was established at the site in 1966, and over the years excavations have continued to add to our knowledge of the mounds and their fascinating treasures. Up to twelve different mounds have been identified on the site, spread over eighty acres in what seems to be a predetermined geometry.

The builders of the Spiro mounds are now known to have been part of the Mississippian culture that flourished from around A.D. 800–1400, specifically a western branch known as the Caddoans. The Caddoan peoples engaged in wide-ranging trade networks that stretched from the Gulf of Mexico to the southwest desert. Their societies were divided into ranks of chiefs, priests, warriors, and a large majority of ordinary farmers. Higher-ranked individuals like chiefs were favored with elaborate burials within mounds like the ones at Spiro, their bones born on litters piled with luxury goods, then covered with dirt. Spiro was a particularly rich and important location because it was situated at a strategic spot on the Arkansas River, which allowed the chiefs to control trade and territory over a wide area.

Although the Spiro Mounds have had more than their share of ghost stories and curses, they also abound in genuine mysteries of this lost civilization that left its mark on the landscape across the southern United States, and about which we still have much to learn.

TAKE ME BACK TO TULSA

- 1934 -

Tulsa

ESCAPING FROM TEXAS AND THE ENMITY OF W. Lee "Pass-the-Biscuits-Pappy" O'Daniel, Bob Wills hoped to make a fresh start in Oklahoma. Since 1931, Wills and his band had been playing for O'Daniel, president of the Burrus Mill, on a Waco radio program advertising the company's flour. The Light Crust Doughboys, as they were then known, had built a substantial following in Texas and surrounding states. Wills and his band mates wanted to capitalize on their success and play dances, which O'Daniel frowned upon. These contract differences and the inevitable personality conflicts between two charismatic men (O'Daniel was soon to be elected governor and U.S. senator from Texas) led to a parting of the ways. When Wills and his band regrouped as Bob Wills and His Playboys, advertising themselves as "formerly the Light Crust Doughboys," O'Daniel sued. The courts ruled in Wills's favor, but Wills could scarcely afford to continue his legal tangles with his former boss. He knew that his band already had many fans in Oklahoma. His decision to try there for a new radio gig in 1934 was the single most important decision of his career.

Oklahoma has an illustrious musical pedigree. Many famous artists, in all genres of music, were born or raised in the state, including Charlie Christian, Gene Autry, Patti Page, Jimmy Rushing, Woody Guthrie, and Leona Mitchell, to name but a few. More recently, artists such as Garth Brooks, Reba McEntire, and Vince Gill have virtually defined contemporary country music. Yet although these performers all share Oklahoma roots, practically all of them made their careers outside of the state, in places like Nashville, New York, Chicago, or Los Angeles. What set Bob Wills and his band apart was that they achieved stardom while living and working in Oklahoma, particularly in Tulsa. There they developed their sound, created their image, gained a national following, and largely invented the style of music known as western swing.

After hitting the road in early 1934, Wills and his band mates tried their luck first in Oklahoma City, only to learn that Pappy O'Daniel wasn't through with them yet. Wills thought that he had struck a deal with local radio station KOMA, but under pressure from O'Daniel, who threatened to withdraw his own program from their schedule, KOMA bowed out. Wills then inquired at another major local station, WKY, where the managers signed them readily. Unfortunately, their stint at WKY lasted only five shows—O'Daniel was able to persuade that station as well to drop them from the line-up. All they had to show for their brief time on Oklahoma City radio was their new full name: Bob Wills and His *Texas* Playboys.

Oklahoma City aside, their big break occurred in Tulsa. Wills and his manager made a call to KVOO, which agreed that very day to give the band a try-out in the unlikely time-slot of midnight to

1:00 A.M. The chance was no doubt a great relief to Wills, who was short of money in the midst of the Depression and had gambled with the livelihoods of his band members and their families. On February 10, 1934, Bob Wills and His Texas Playboys made their first broadcast from KVOO, which would continue to carry their show—in more favorable time-slots—until 1942. The signal from the powerful AM station could be heard as far away as California. O'Daniel made one last attempt to squelch the show, but to no avail. The station management at last stood up to him.

Locally, the popularity of Wills and his band grew rapidly as they hired themselves out for dances in towns and cities across the state. They began their long association with Tulsa's legendary Cain's Ballroom, known then as Cain's Dancing Academy, in 1935. With a wink at Pappy O'Daniel, they marketed their own brand of "Play Boy" flour, which had brisk sales in the mid-1930s. Wills purchased radio time in order to have the best possible exposure for his band and his brand. He also packaged himself and his fellow band members very shrewdly, purchasing a ranch near Tulsa where all of the Playboys kept and rode horses. Giving up the sweaters and ties of their Light Crust Doughboys years, they began to dress for performances in western garb and cowboy hats.

The warm folksiness, versatility, and skill of the Texas Playboys proved to be irresistible to both radio and live audiences. Large dance crowds (of 1,000 to 2,000) were not unusual when Wills and his band played even in small towns—a remarkable tribute to their drawing power, considering that times were hard and money scarce. According to Wills's biographer, the Texas Playboys had an incredible repertoire of over 3,600 songs, so there was always something for everyone, and no two shows were ever alike. They frequently were asked to perform at funerals (for which Wills charged no fee), and they were the featured performers at one governor's inauguration.

As the magnetic center of the Texas Playboys, with his trademark "hollering" and fiddle-playing, Wills carried much of the burden of promoting and sustaining the band. It was a job that he relished, yet it also took its toll on him during the Tulsa years. Wills first arrived in Tulsa back in 1934 with a wife and child, but the marriage ended in divorce in 1935. Between that year and 1942, he was married again no less than five times, suffered from depression, and had a serious drinking problem. Remarkably, despite the uproar in his personal life, all of it seemed to fall away when Wills and his band took the stage. The popularity of the Texas Playboys only grew throughout the Tulsa years, culminating in their 1940 recording of the song, "New San Antonio Rose." This song was their first big hit, extending their appeal from the Southwest to fans nationwide and earning a gold record. It also led to a Hollywood movie contract for Wills and several band members.

World War II cut short the Tulsa era of the Texas Playboys. Several members of the band were drafted or enlisted, as was Bob Wills himself. Some months before the break-up, the Texas Playboys had recorded what would become one of their classics, "Take Me Back to Tulsa." After his stint in the army, Wills moved both his family and available band members out to California. Nevertheless, Tulsa had left its imprint on him, just as Bob Wills and His Texas Playboys left their imprint on American popular music.

BLACK SUNDAY

- 1935 -

Cimarron County

EVEN BEFORE THAT DAY WHEN IT APPEARED THE world was about to end, people in the Panhandle were meeting regularly to pray for rain. The drought had lasted four years and was not yet half over. In Cimarron County, ground zero of the Dust Bowl, the last good wheat crop had been in 1931. Since then, the wheat made next to nothing, or nothing at all. Now it was 1935, and during the last week of March, a single dust storm rolled across Oklahoma and blew away one-quarter of the wheat that had been planted. And still the wind kept blowing, and no rains came.

March and April of 1935 were particularly bad months in the Dust Bowl region, which had already witnessed dust storms by the dozen in previous years. Dust was thick in the air for almost seven weeks, although some days were worse than others. Fifteen storms lasted more than twenty-four hours each, and four storms each lasted more than two days. People in Cimarron County and other areas of the Panhandle thought they had seen everything. On Wednesday, April 11, what was described as the worst dust storm ever to hit Oklahoma blasted across the state. In downtown Oklahoma City, visibility fell to two blocks, and signs could barely be read. But things were worse to the northwest, in the direction of the Panhandle. There, because of the choking dust, people could not see from one room to another. Yes, this was the worst that people had seen—until April 14, 1935, which became known as Black Sunday. Black Sunday gave the Dust Bowl its name.

Many years afterward, residents in places like Beaver, Guymon, Tyrone, and Hooker would remember what happened to them on that day. There were actually worse years for dust storms, if one were making a count; 1937 was probably the most severe for those living in the Panhandle. Yet there was something different about the Black Sunday storm, perhaps because it was Palm Sunday, or perhaps because the day had dawned so blue and clear. Temperatures were rising into the low eighties, and the sun was shining. After church, people packed picnic baskets or went out for Sunday drives. It was that kind of day.

The storm front arrived in northern Oklahoma at about 4:00 P.M., stretching 1,000 miles across several states, driven by upper-level winds of over 100 mph. When it arrived at Beaver, the temperature fell from eighty degrees to sixty-three in fifteen minutes, and then kept dropping rapidly toward the thirties. Winds of over fifty miles per hour buffeted everything in their path, hurling gravel through windows. And with the wind came the dust—thick, dark red silt from some unlucky denuded farmlands to the north. Within minutes, total darkness descended on what had been a pleasant, sunny afternoon.

From a distance, the black dust storm looked like something worse than dust, like something almost biblical. Some compared it to the smoke from burning oil. As they saw the huge, roiling black wall approach, people ran for their cellars. One couple who had been out on a drive took refuge with a stranger in her cellar when they saw the storm nearing them. When they emerged after the storm, they thought the brunt had passed, and found dust piled throughout the woman's house. The couple continued in the darkness toward their own farm, but had to stop from time to time because they could not even see the radiator cap at the end of their car's hood. Once they worried that they had driven off the road, and stopped to feel their way toward the fence posts they presumed were alongside it. They gave up the idea when they realized they were losing sight of their car just a short distance away and, without a rope, might become lost. Indeed, another story told of a man who wandered a ten-acre garden plot for eight hours before being found. Others claimed that they could not see their hand in front of their face.

In Guymon, the Methodists had gathered in their church to pray for rain when the black cloud hit. The minister's wife had already spent a good part of the morning cleaning the dust from previous storms out of the pews to prepare for the Sunday services. That afternoon, the church was full when darkness suddenly descended. The altar could not be seen from the pews, but some made their way to it to pray more fervently. A few lay in the aisles certain that the end-time had arrived.

Perhaps the most unusual event interrupted on Black Sunday was the rabbit-drive at Tyrone, in Texas County. A large number of people had gathered to flush out the pesky jackrabbits that had invaded gardens and crops and that provided a source of meat. Spreading out in a long line and carrying strong sticks, they were driving the rabbits from their cover to trap them against a fence. A good time was being had by all, but when the rabbit-drovers were within fifty feet of the fence and could see hundreds of rabbits swarming in front of them, the black pall of dust arrived. People fled to their cars, and most of the rabbits escaped. Later, many rabbits, birds, and other animals were found choked to death by the dust. Automobiles also stalled throughout the area, their engines fouled.

Humans did not fare too well in the dust clouds, either. Doctors had made note of the increasing occurrence of "dust pneumonia" in the Dust Bowl region, and an epidemic of it occurred in the aftermath of Black Sunday. Those stricken were brought to hospitals and doctors' offices, coughing up mud. It is not known how many people may have succumbed to the pneumonia in Oklahoma, but hospitals in one Kansas county adjacent to the Panhandle reported thirty-three dead.

The dust storms of the 1930s were awesome, destructive spectacles. The largest could engulf several states at once, throwing millions of tons of topsoil thousands of feet into the atmosphere and blowing it out to ships at sea in the Atlantic. Scientists later estimated the dust storms of 1935 had removed 850 million tons of soil from the Dust Bowl region. It is amazing that anyone could long endure such an environmental catastrophe, and in fact, Cimarron County lost 40 percent of its population during the decade. The Panhandle as a whole lost nearly one-third of its population. Those who left moved to nearby states and cities or joined the Okie exodus to California. Those who remained held on long enough to watch the rains return at last, beginning in the late 1930s and early 1940s. The Panhandle became a productive agricultural region once again, and improved farming techniques, soil conservation measures, and government subsidies helped the farmers there weather the dust storms which came in later decades.

MEET THE OKIES

- 1939 -

Route 66

IN OKLAHOMA, EVERY SCHOOL KID KNOWS that John Steinbeck got it all wrong in *The Grapes of Wrath*. His research in the state consisted primarily of driving across it on Route 66. At the beginning of the story, he makes much of drought and dust, despite the fact that the Joad family's farm is located near Sallisaw, which is hundreds of miles away from the actual Dust Bowl region. The Joads are poor farm workers who move a lot, occasionally use off-color language, and breastfeed total strangers. Most people in 1930s Oklahoma were not like that.

Steinbeck's electrifying 1939 novel, along with the John Ford movie released the following year, brought the Okies to national awareness and turned them indelibly into a stereotype. But who were the Okies, really? As in *The Grapes of Wrath*, most of their story is usually told after their arrival in California. But where did they come from in Oklahoma, and why did they leave?

The Great Depression hit all of America hard during the 1930s, yet it landed on Oklahoma with exceptional severity. Oklahoma as a homesteader's frontier had not quite panned out. By 1930, nearly two-thirds of Oklahoma's farmers were tenants—not landowners or homeowners, but renters. Most of these tenant farm families lived in the cotton belt of the eastern half of the state—Steinbeck had that much of it correct. This rootless population moved frequently by habit, constantly seeking a better situation. Almost half of them changed location each year, though they commonly remained in the general vicinity. Their situation was precarious in the best of times, and the times were far from the best. In fact, falling crop prices during the 1920s led hundreds of thousands to leave the state even before the Depression occurred. Most of these migrants went to surrounding states, but some wound up in California as well. They were Okies before Okies had a name.

The Depression did not help matters for the tenants. The increasing use of tractors by landowners—Steinbeck got that part right—along with government programs to reduce the amount of land in cultivation led hundreds of thousands more people to take to the road. Extensive floods rather than drought also played a role in pushing people off the land, particularly in 1937. The most surprising fact about the Okie migration of the 1930s, however, is that the majority of the migrants were not tenant farmers. Somewhat more than half who left the state came from small towns and cities; they were small businessmen, workers, and others whose livelihoods had disappeared because of hard times. Like the tenants, many of these migrants tried their luck first in another town or city within Oklahoma. The result was the spread of numerous ramshackle camps known as Hoovervilles, such as those that sprang up along the North Canadian River in Oklahoma City. Many of the makeshift shelters in the Hoovervilles were made from cardboard, and conditions became so dire during the early 1930s that city officials finally took the situation in hand, bulldozing them after constructing public housing elsewhere in the city for those displaced. Yet such measures were far from sufficient to accommodate the growing numbers of migrants, and so people had to cast their lot outside the state.

Determining just how many people left Oklahoma, and how many of those arrived in California, is difficult because the term "Okie" was used to insult migrants from all states indiscriminately. What is known is rather staggering: Oklahoma had a net loss of 440,000 people from its population between 1930 and 1940, close to 20 percent—the most of any state in the region. The state's population would not exceed its official 1920 level again until the 1970 census. Of the roughly half-million migrants, only about 2 or 3 percent appear to have been from the Dust Bowl area proper; "Dust Bowl refugee" was definitely a misconception. But the preponderance of Oklahomans among the arrivals in California was no mistake. During a survey taken after 1935, over one-quarter of the total were identified as being from Oklahoma alone, as many as 75,000 people in the second half of the decade.

In light of these cold, hard facts, Oklahoma's adverse reaction to the publication of *The Grapes of Wrath* is less than surprising. In the land of progress, such things were not supposed to happen. State officials, chambers of commerce, and other boosters rallied to dispel what they saw as an obscene slur against the state's image, but their efforts availed little against a literary masterpiece (winning Steinbeck both a Pulitzer and a Nobel prize) and its Oscar-winning film adaptation. Within months of the book's release, the most famous Okie of them all, Woody Guthrie, went onstage in New York City and began singing of his experiences to a national audience.

Ironically, for all of the bluster of the state's defenders, *The Grapes of Wrath* flew off the shelves in Oklahoma. It remained a bestseller within the state for years after its release, second only to the block-buster *Gone With the Wind*. Libraries could not keep enough copies, and waiting lists hundreds of names long formed. One bookstore claimed to have sold over 1,000 copies, and another bookstore owner remarked that people who appeared never to have bought a book before were coming to the store to buy it.

This amount of publicity did help to improve the lot of Okies and other migrants in California, which had been less than welcoming to those they saw as undesirables. The Okies had been compared to a plague of locusts, and their labor camps were called "little Oklahomas." An anti-migrant law had also been passed in the state legislature. The federal government intervened to build better camps for the migrant workers, and the Supreme Court overturned the anti-migrant law. But more than anything else, the coming of World War II reversed the fortunes of the Okies in their new home. Now labor on the farm and in the factories was in high demand, and suddenly they were "desirables."

The final irony of the great Okie migration is that many of the transplants took root and flourished in California at places such as Bakersfield in the San Joaquin Valley, which became a true "little Oklahoma." The migrants and their descendants brought along their Baptist and Pentecostal faiths, their taste for chicken-fried steak, their twangy accents, and their distinctive music, all of which could still be found in Bakersfield down to the 1990s. The most famous son of Bakersfield, Merle Haggard, was also the son of Okies. Even though he was California-born and -raised, Haggard could still sing with conviction of his Okie pride.

KATE AND ANGIE

- 1941 -

Muskogee

IN DECEMBER OF 1909, REPORTS SURFACED OF three "elf" children living in a hollow tree near Muskogee. The details of the story were far from charming, however. The children were Cherokee orphans who begged food from nearby farms and drank water from streams. Their hair was thickly matted with dirt. It took several weeks to locate their guardian, who on investigation was found to be availing himself of royalty money from oil properties that the homeless children owned. The man was also the "guardian"—in a legal sense only—for fifty-one other Native American children.

There are crimes that are so disgraceful that their stories cannot be told. The guilty must enforce silence at all costs. Careers or reputations are ruined, and sometimes lives are lost. Such was the case with the story of the Indian land scandals of the early 1900s. Two courageous Oklahoma women, Kate Barnard and Angie Debo, risked everything in order to investigate the scandals, and to bring to light and justice one of the state's dirty secrets.

Beginning in the late 1880s, the federal government undertook the complex process of breaking up the tribal domains of the native peoples it had removed and relocated to Indian Territory. Over the next two decades or so, members of different tribes and nations were each conveyed their own allotment of land as a way of fostering in them habits of free enterprise and individual initiative. On the surface, the process was meant to bring about a transition and "assimilation" of Native Americans from older, communal ways of living toward a more modern, mainstream American way of life. Yet a by-product of the allotment process—or perhaps, its main goal—was that it freed up a huge "surplus" of land that was once tribally owned, and ultimately made it available for white settlement. It also made property-owners of thousands of isolated, illiterate full-blood Indians, as well as children and others who knew little about or lacked the means of protecting their own interests. They were ripe pickings for unscrupulous men, some of them in high places.

As farmland, the allotments were valuable enough, but with the discovery of oil, the lust for Indian land became frenzied. Federal law was supposed to safeguard the allotments; the land was not allowed to be "alienable" or sellable for many years. But there were ways around these types of restrictions, as scandal after scandal showed. Some resorted to outright forgery, faking names on very liberal leases. Others used real names but the individuals in question never knew their land was being leased. An allotment could be willed to another person in some circumstances, and elderly Native Americans were preyed upon for this very purpose. Also, individuals could ask Congress to release their land from the restrictions on sale, which thousands of Indians did, often after cajolery or coercion. And a favorite means to gain control of allotments was through guardianship, not only of underage children, but also of adults.

In 1908, this particular scam was made all the easier when authority over the holdings of minors was transferred by federal officials to county probate courts. Now, forty local judges had responsibility for more than 60,000 children (with and without parents) who owned lands estimated to be worth over $150 million. These judges were often more than happy to help out their land-hungry friends and associates. One of these bogus guardians had control of the assets of 350 children. It was how he made his living; somehow, his legal fees took virtually all the income that their lands earned. More and more stories came to light of the consequences for the children, like the young Chickasaw orphan girl whose guardian was boarding her with a family for ten dollars per month and not sending her to school, while her thousand-acre allotment was earning him $2,500 annually—a very good income in the early 1900s.

Kate Barnard became involved especially because of the treatment of the orphans. She was the state commissioner of charities and corrections, a passionate, strong-willed person with a piercing voice who was the first woman elected to statewide office. Barnard advocated for children, poor people, labor unions, people with disabilities, and prison inmates, putting her at odds with Oklahoma's power-brokers, including William H. "Alfalfa Bill" Murray. She claimed to have discovered the three Cherokee children living in the tree—and personally cut their hair. Barnard took up the cause of the Indian orphans and pushed for a broader mandate to intervene on behalf of any Native American, young or old, whose land was being pilfered. Eventually she was able to hire a lawyer named J. H. Stolper to bring cases against the sham guardians. By 1912, he had recovered over $1 million of the orphans' money and a number of the guardians had been successfully prosecuted.

Yet there were political costs to this crusade, devastating costs. The local courthouse rings were part of the machinery of the reigning Democratic Party; more than a few prominent state politicians had done well off of Indian lands themselves. In 1913, legislators began to investigate Barnard's office and forced the resignation of Stolper. In 1914, they cut her appropriations to the extent that she could not afford to buy stamps, much less pay the salaries of attorneys or inspectors. She personally borrowed money to try to keep her office open. The partisan press turned on her and depicted her as frivolous and mentally unstable. Her health, always frail, suffered a collapse, and she was finished in Oklahoma politics by 1915. Only five years earlier, she had been the most popular figure, man or woman, in state government. Barnard lived until 1930 in obscurity, spending the final years of her life in a hotel in downtown Oklahoma City. She had hoped someday to write a memoir of her role in early state political history, but the project was never completed. She died at the age of fifty-four.

Fortunately, Barnard's story did not remain unknown, particularly as it related to the Indian land scandals. Within only two years of Barnard's passing, Angie Debo, a historian in her thirties who had just published her first book, began a new project: a history of the allotment process in Oklahoma. As a teenager Debo had once heard Barnard speak and been impressed by her force and charisma. Barnard's efforts to save the Indian orphans from despoliation—including the story of the three Cherokee children in the tree—became part of the intricate narrative of Debo's book *And Still the Waters Run: The Betrayal of the Five Civilized Tribes*.

Although now recognized as a classic, *And Still the Waters Run* almost did not see publication, a tale that has itself become part of its legend. Later generations have come to view Debo as something like the patron saint of Oklahoma, but at the time she was an unknown scholar of history. In that era, too, women had a difficult time being taken seriously in academia. Debo submitted the manuscript to the University of Oklahoma Press, and by 1937, it appeared about to be published. But some pre-publication reviewers had given warnings about the revelations in the book, that it named the names of men whom the university did not want to upset. Fearing political consequences, the press editor, Joseph Brandt, bowed to pressure from the university president not to publish the book.

Only in 1941 did *And Still the Waters Run* see publication, at another university press outside the state where Brandt had since become editor. The whole history of the widespread exploitation of Native Americans during the formative years of Oklahoma was now known in irrefutable detail. And the story of how Kate Barnard, the "Good Angel of Oklahoma," tried to defend the weakest and most vulnerable was finally told.

FREAKS OF THE STORM

- 1948 -

Tinker Air Force Base

DURING THE TORNADO THAT STRUCK FAIRFAX ON the night of February 27, 1918, Mrs. James Ford and her child were rushing to a storm cellar when they were killed by a falling oil derrick. It was a curiously symbolic Oklahoma moment, mingling violent weather, oil, and proneness to tragedy.

Like the derricks and pumpjacks that were once so typical of Oklahoma's landscape, tornadoes have defined the state's image throughout its history, and with good reason: over the past several decades, no other place on earth has experienced so many powerful twisters. Stories such as Mrs. Ford's have been sadly common. The newspapers used to call them "freaks of the storm."

At the height of the tornado that destroyed much of Snyder, Oklahoma, on May 10, 1905, a Colonel Williamson is said to have ushered a woman whom he thought was his wife to a place of safety, only to discover that he was mistaken. Later he found his wife at the makeshift morgue, her head severed from her body. On May 20, 1910, in the ferocious storm that struck Pauls Valley, two children were seriously injured when pieces of debris actually penetrated the roof of the storm cellar where they had thought themselves protected. Three decades later, on March 20, 1948, during the historic tornado that demolished dozens of planes at Tinker Air Force Base, one witness recalled seeing a P-47 fly by, low to the ground—without a pilot.

Oklahoma's weather history is rife with such bizarre incidents, but the descent of tornadoes into ordinary lives may be equally as poignant. On May 31, 1947, the Zimmermans of Leedey, Oklahoma, returned home from a visit to a nearby town to find the convertible they had left in their driveway wrapped around a tree and an empty foundation where their house had once stood. A reporter followed them through the scattered debris while they looked for keepsakes or anything salvageable. Mrs. Zimmerman, dazed, clutched a sock that her son had outgrown and a broken piece from a chest of drawers.

The sheer number of Oklahoma's tornadoes, each chaotic and unpredictable, must tend to produce some percentage of oddities, tragedies, and miracles. Yet certain storms stand out by their magnitude and destructiveness. The Blackwell tornado of May 25, 1955, which killed twenty people, entered the town wreathed in lightning. At least 40 percent of the population of Snyder was killed or injured by the storm that claimed Colonel Williamson's wife in 1905, and an estimated 95 percent of the town's buildings were destroyed. The Woodward tornado of April 9, 1947 remains to this day the deadliest, with 107 killed; it was memorable as well for the snowfall that occurred afterward. Also never to be forgotten was the huge tornado outbreak of May 3, 1999, which featured the most powerful windspeeds ever measured on earth: 318 mph.

As the long-suffering epicenter of such disasters, Oklahoma has also been home to many historic advances in understanding, predicting, and surviving tornadoes. The first widely published photograph of a tornado was taken in 1896 at Oklahoma City. The first 16mm movie footage of a tornado was captured in 1951 near the town of Corn. But perhaps most historically important, in the aftermath of the 1948 twister that struck Tinker Air Force Base, Major Ernest Fawbush and Captain Robert Miller issued the world's first tornado forecast, successfully predicting several hours beforehand the second tornado to strike the facility in the space of five days—a freak occurrence in itself. Fawbush and Miller had spent many hours after the first twister poring over massive amounts of data in an effort to determine what conditions had spawned the March 20th storm and earlier storms. When they saw that very much the same conditions were forming again on March 25, the two weathermen contacted the commanding officer at Tinker, Major General Fred S. Borum. Fawbush and Miller were reluctant to predict that another tornado might actually hit the air force base again, which would have been virtually unprecedented. Yet the data pointed to the real possibility, and when pressed hard by Borum, the two men finally gave a definite answer. Borum ordered them to notify the base, and they did so by 2:50 P.M. The tornado struck at 5:58 P.M., initially hitting the same building that had been the first one damaged on March 20. Although more planes were destroyed—there were some 2,000 parked at the base, so it was hard to miss them—Borum had been given enough time to take precautions and limit some of the damage.

The technique of tornado forecasting developed by Fawbush and Miller proved to be impressively accurate. During a period of fourteen months between 1949 and 1950, they issued thirty-four forecasts, and a tornado formed in thirty-one of those instances. At that time the civilian National Weather Service did not yet issue tornado alerts to the public, but forecasts from Tinker were publicized unofficially by local radio stations for several years thereafter. Only after intense public and political pressure did the National Weather Service, less sure of its methods than the air force, begin to issue its own tornado alerts in 1952.

The Weather Service, too, came to realize the value of Oklahoma as a premier location to study weather phenomena, establishing the National Severe Storms Laboratory (NSSL) with its headquarters at Norman. Since its creation the NSSL has been on the leading edge of research in tornadic formation and behavior and has served as an important testing ground for new weather technology. The world's first genuinely scientific "storm chase" (popularized in the movie *Twister*) was staged from the NSSL in 1961. A decade or so later, at Union City on May 24, 1973, storm chasers from the NSSL and the University of Oklahoma recorded the entire life cycle of a tornado from beginning to end, formulating the definitive stages of tornadic development. The NSSL has also been in the forefront of Doppler radar technology, making the first Doppler observations of a severe storm supercell in 1972, and, beginning in 1989, employing portable units set up by chase teams to probe the complex conditions within tornadoes from a distance of only a mile or two. Most recently, scientists at the NSSL have been experimenting with a new type of radar called "phased array," which will allow them to gather information on a storm much more rapidly than conventional methods.

Since the first daring attempts by Fawbush and Miller, all of these advances have improved the ability of forecasters to warn the public of oncoming storms, and no doubt they have saved many lives. But nature never loses its capacity to astonish, especially in Oklahoma.

VISIBLE AT LAST

- 1950 -

Norman

GEORGE W. MCLAURIN WAS AN UNLIKELY GRAD SCHOOL applicant. He was sixty-one years old and already retired as a college professor. He was also a black man seeking admission to a whites-only university— the University of Oklahoma (OU).

It is often remarked that historically, race relations in Oklahoma were relatively mild compared to those of the Deep South states. It is true that African Americans comprised a smaller percentage of the population in Oklahoma than in other states of the former Confederacy, posing less of a threat to the ruling whites. Some observers, like the novelist Ralph Ellison, also thought that Oklahoma's status as a young state, not far removed from its days as a frontier, had instilled blacks living there with more hope and independence than in the South. Yet Oklahoma had witnessed such horrific incidents as the Tulsa Race Riot of 1921, and segregation had a prominent place in the state constitution. When the war against Nazi Germany called into question racism everywhere, black Oklahomans prepared to challenge the status quo that for too long had limited their freedom and opportunities, as well as their self-respect.

McLaurin was one of several concerned students and educators who had come forward after a prior attempt to overthrow segregation in higher education, the Ada Lois Sipuel case, had been stymied by actions of the state government. In 1946, Sipuel, a graduate of all-black Langston University, had sought admittance to the University of Oklahoma law school, and she had gone to court against the state board of regents when she was refused. A district court and the state supreme court ruled against her, but the U.S. Supreme Court found in her favor: the state did not provide equal facilities for the study of law for both blacks and whites. But rather than simply admit Sipuel to the OU College of Law, the regents quickly threw together a separate "Langston University School of Law" for her, in the basement of the state capitol, claiming that it would provide her with an equally good professional education.

In light of this trickery by the state, lawyers for the NAACP, including future Supreme Court justice Thurgood Marshall, developed a strategy whereby a number of black applicants would attempt to enter a range of professional programs; the state government could not possibly afford to create new and separate programs in all areas. George McLaurin applied for the doctoral program in education at OU, while others applied at the engineering and pharmacy schools. When McLaurin was rejected because of his race, he filed suit in federal court, which upheld his contention that the state was required to provide him with doctoral courses. Yet since the state could not keep duplicating professional schools, legislators hastily passed a law allowing McLaurin to attend OU education classes on a segregated basis. University president George Lynn Cross, while sympathetic to both Sipuel and McLaurin and helpful behind the scenes, nevertheless implemented the letter of the new law.

What McLaurin next experienced at OU revealed the absurdity of racial segregation for all to see. In one of his classes, he was required to sit in an anteroom (sometimes called a broom closet) and crane his neck to see his instructor. For a time he was denied access to the beautiful Great Reading Room in the university library; instead, he had to sit in an outer area behind stacks of newspapers to conceal his presence. His meals were scheduled at different times and at separate tables from white students in the cafeteria. He was even assigned one of two toilets in a building, leaving the other for all of the white male students to use. When there were complaints from incensed white students about McLaurin's treatment, the administration gave in somewhat, yet only up to a point. He was allowed to sit in the same classroom as other students if he stayed in a separate area, usually roped-off with a "Reserved for Colored" sign over it. He could eat at the same time as whites in the cafeteria or study with them in the reading room, but only at his own table.

Marshall and the NAACP again filed suit on McLaurin's behalf in federal court, asserting that these conditions were blatantly unequal. This time, the federal court ruling went against them, and they took the case to the U.S. Supreme Court. On June 5, 1950, the court issued its decision in *George W. McLaurin v. Oklahoma Board of Regents for Higher Education*. The justices ruled that through their various measures to separate McLaurin, the regents had violated the equal protection clause of the Fourteenth Amendment. They had "handicapped" McLaurin's ability to interact with his peers and gain a useful education. Black professional students were entitled to equal treatment in educational institutions, the court ruled unanimously.

Oklahoma legislators and officials had already begun revising the state's segregation laws even before the *McLaurin* decision was handed down. The number of African American applicants at OU and other state schools had become too burdensome for university administrators to cope with, and by the end of 1949, there were twenty-three black students attending the University of Oklahoma. Ada Lois Sipuel (now Fisher) herself was admitted to the law school and graduated in 1951. Beyond ushering in this immediate progress, the *McLaurin* case also helped to set the stage for the Supreme Court's landmark *Brown v. Board of Education* ruling in 1954, which declared that separate educational facilities were inherently unequal. The justices specifically cited their earlier reasoning in the *McLaurin* case to justify their broader decision in the Brown lawsuit, which affected public schools across the southern United States.

In the spirit of Fisher and McLaurin, Oklahomans continued to remain in the forefront as the civil rights movement gained momentum during the 1950s. In 1952, Ralph Ellison published his masterpiece, *Invisible Man,* which was inspired in part by his experiences growing up in Oklahoma City during the 1910s and 1920s. The influential novel explored the experience of African Americans reduced to ciphers by racial prejudices that refused to see them as individual human beings—an eye-opening book for many white readers. And in 1958, Clara Luper and numerous black students in Oklahoma City made themselves quite visible by launching some of the movement's first sit-ins of segregated restaurants, challenging the social segregation that still persisted.

Thanks to the courageous actions of Luper and her predecessors, Oklahoma and the nation as a whole at last began to live up to the ideals of freedom and equality for all. In 2001, this key role of Oklahomans in the civil rights struggle was finally recognized when Bizzell Memorial Library at the University of Oklahoma, where George McLaurin had once been banished to his lonely study table, was designated as a National Historic Landmark.

BLACK SATURDAY

- 1957 -

Norman

IT IS OFTEN SAID THAT COLLEGE FOOTBALL IS A RELIGION in Oklahoma, although the same observation might apply to Nebraska, Texas, Alabama, or any number of other states. Armchair social critics point somewhat dubiously to the rise of the University of Oklahoma dynasty as reviving the collective self-esteem of a state buffeted by the Dust Bowl and the Depression. Sports writers and historians like to note the strange coincidence of the state's fiftieth anniversary celebration and the end of the Oklahoma Sooners' record winning-streak on the very same day, November 16, 1957. Could there be some mysterious connection between the fortunes of Sooner football and the Sooner State?

The forty-seven-game streak that was compiled by teams under head coach Bud Wilkinson has never been bested among Division I-A schools. After losing the season opener and tying the next game in 1953, the Sooners defeated Texas on October 10 and did not lose another game until that fateful November weekend in 1957. In fact, not one of the players on the 1957 OU team had ever lost a collegiate game. Sooner teams won two Orange Bowl trophies in the process and were ranked as national champions in 1954 and 1956. During the course of the streak, OU averaged over thirty-four points per game, while its opponents scored on average just under six.

The phenomenal success of the 1950s Sooners has been ascribed largely to Wilkinson, a fatherly, dedicated, imperturbable man who as a coach was highly organized and methodical, yet innovative. Wilkinson perfected the split-T formation and is credited with inventing the no-huddle offense. He oversaw an earlier thirty-one game winning streak from 1948 to 1950 and a national championship in 1950. His teams did not lose a conference game for an astounding thirteen years. Halfback Billy Vessels won the Heisman Trophy in 1952, and in 1956 Wilkinson made a place at fullback for Prentice Gautt, the first African American to start for the Sooners—years ahead of many college teams in the South. Meanwhile, off the field, Sooner players graduated at a rate of over 90 percent during much of Wilkinson's tenure. He was, in many ways, the consummate college football coach.

The Sooners and their fans had thus begun the 1957 season full of confidence that Wilkinson would again lead them through another flawless year. But even before November 16, there were warning signs that OU might be faltering. On October 26, the Sooners barely eked out a victory over Colorado in Norman, 14-13—a game that the Golden Buffaloes led going into the fourth quarter. The following week Oklahoma hardly looked dominating at Kansas State, but did come away from a muddy field with a 13-0 victory. The Sooners seemed to have regained their footing in a 39-14 win over Missouri on November 9 at Columbia, which earned them the conference title and a trip to the Orange Bowl. There was inevitably a loss of motivation after achieving these important goals, however, and during the ensuing week the players found it difficult to muster themselves for their next opponent, Notre Dame—a team they had trounced at home in South Bend the previous season, 40-0. For Saturday's game, the Sooners were pegged a three-touchdown favorite.

The Fighting Irish, for their part, had no problems with preparation or motivation. According to one account, they had infiltrated a spy to observe OU practice sessions a few days prior to the game. Moreover, it was intimidating to the Notre Dame players that the state of Oklahoma was full of anti-Catholic bigots—an overstatement, but not without foundation in that era. It seems that they had received some gibes from Sooner fans and players in their devastating loss a year earlier, and smarting from those memories, the Irish arrived in Norman at a high pitch. On Black Saturday, the Sooners were tending business, but the Fighting Irish were on a mission.

OU coaches and players may have underestimated the significance of the game, but fans had not. A record crowd of over 63,000 filled Memorial Stadium, including 8,000 Notre Dame supporters. The game was nationally televised by NBC and watched by an estimated thirty million viewers. For most of the afternoon, the weather was partly cloudy and blustery, with temperatures in the fifties: perfect conditions for football, with no excuses.

The game quickly took shape as a defensive struggle. Fifty-six minutes ran off the clock before either team scored. Twice in the first half, the Sooners made successful goal-line stands against the Irish, who in turn thwarted three good scoring opportunities by OU. The two teams combined for less than one hundred yards offense in the first half, which ended in a scoreless tie. The second half proceeded much like the first until a minute or so into the fourth quarter, when Notre Dame received a punt in the end zone and began grinding out an eighty-yard drive from their own twenty-yard line. A fumble occurred in Oklahoma territory, but the Irish recovered it. Running on virtually every play, the Irish pushed down to fourth-and-goal at the OU three-yard line, and the Sooner defense seemed about to snuff out yet another Notre Dame drive. The roar of the crowd was deafening at that point, and the Irish quarterback, Bob Williams, could not call signals to his teammates. Several OU players motioned to the fans for quiet, and the noise-level subsided. On the next play, Williams pitched to halfback Dick Lynch, who ran around end and in for the touchdown.

After the Irish kicked their extra point, the Sooners had less than four minutes to play for a tie (the two-point conversion was not approved for college football until several years later). Now there was another national record at stake: the Sooners had scored at least once in 112 consecutive games. Wilkinson, probably as stunned by the turn of events as many OU fans, made a series of questionable calls, sending in substitutes for first-string players, in a desperate attempt to change the Sooners' momentum. The gamble seemed to work at first, and Oklahoma found itself in Notre Dame territory at the twenty-three with a minute remaining. But a pass into the end zone was intercepted by the Irish, who then ran out the clock. The winning streak and the scoring streak were over.

Oklahoma fans remained in the stands for many minutes, unable to comprehend what had happened. The OU locker room was silent, and Wilkinson tried to offer some consoling words. Some OU players wept, and one later compared the experience to death. Others accepted the defeat with more equanimity, crossing the stadium to the Notre Dame locker room and offering their congratulations. They respected the fact that they had simply been outplayed. Wilkinson took full responsibility.

Across the state, the mood was somber and resigned. Some spoke bravely of starting a new streak. Restaurants were full on Saturday evening, but conversations were strangely muted. At the Oklahoma City Golf and Country Club, a victory dance went on as scheduled, but somehow it wasn't the same.

Many analysts believe that the record forty-seven-game winning streak will never be broken. The pressures of big-time college sports, awash now in money and media attention, have become too great.

WAY DOWN YONDER

- 1972 -

Anadarko Basin

IN THE NINETEENTH CENTURY AT A PLACE called Boyd Springs, the Chickasaw Indians had only to force a pipe or gun barrel into the ground to tap a natural gas pocket just below the surface. The easy source of heat and light made the oil springs a favorite spot to camp.

Later, during the early days of Oklahoma's first oil strikes, natural gas often went to waste. There was relatively little market for it, and only a few tanks or pipelines existed to capture and transport it. Millions of cubic feet of gas would daily be vented from oil wells to no purpose. And sometimes, if the weather conditions were right, the gas would collect in low-lying areas. The careless toss of a cigar or the spark of a car engine could cause a massive explosion; in fact, one such accident killed two men innocently driving past the Cushing Oil Field during its heyday.

In time, of course, natural gas came to be considered much more than a novelty or a nuisance. Oilmen changed their thinking about the role of gas in crude oil production, and they began to conserve it. By World War II, gas was sought in Oklahoma and elsewhere as an important energy source. Much of this development hinged on technological advances in pipelines and storage facilities, able now to bring gas to the millions of new homes and expanding industries of the postwar economic boom. Government regulation of gas prices made it relatively cheap to consume, and Americans did so, by the billions of cubic feet.

In the 1960s and 1970s, as worries over an impending energy crisis loomed, new reserves of natural gas began to be scouted. One of the pioneers in this effort was Oklahoman Robert Hefner III. The son and grandson of oilmen, Hefner became intrigued by the subsurface geology of a 12,000-square-mile area in western Oklahoma and the Texas Panhandle known as the Anadarko Basin. He was convinced of the possibility that immense reserves of gas might reside there deep underground, as many as 3 miles deep and beyond. Most experts scoffed at the idea, but Hefner persisted. He and some partners formed an independent exploration firm, the GHK Companies, and began drilling their first ultra-deep wells in the basin. Their first successful effort, "No. 1 Green," was spudded (or started) in 1967, yet it required two years to reach what was then a record depth of 24,473 feet. The well did find gas in plenty, but because of price controls, the sale of the gas could not cover the high cost of drilling so deeply ($6.5 million, as opposed to a few hundred thousand dollars for a conventional shallow well).

Hefner's conundrum was the conundrum of the Anadarko Basin as a whole: the natural gas was down there, but it was too expensive to bring it up. GHK, in tandem with Lone Star Producing Company, continued to drill wildcat (or prospecting) wells in hopes that the economic equation would change. Another well, called E. R. Baden No.1, reached a world-record depth of 30,050 feet in 1972 at a location near Elk City. A huge drilling rig was required, practically a deep-sea drilling platform on land. The steel pipe alone that went into the Baden No. 1 well weighed over 1.2 million pounds.

Hefner and his associates learned a good deal from the Baden well, which they proceeded to apply to their next, most renowned project: the Bertha Rogers No. 1. Located south of Burns Flat in Washita County, the Bertha Rogers pushed the technological envelope even further. An extra-large-diameter pipe was manufactured especially for the well; at its fullest extent, including the cement that was used in the drilling process, 1.45 million pounds of this pipe had to be supported by the rig. Drilling began on November 12, 1972, and lasted until 1974, averaging sixty feet per day, until stopping ultimately at 31,441 feet deep. It was the deepest hole in the world until it was surpassed by a well in the Soviet Union several years later. Even so, the Bertha Rogers reigned as the deepest well in the United States for three decades, finally exceeded in 2004.

Conditions are quite hostile that far down into the earth's crust. Temperatures reach 500 degrees, and pressures run up to 24,000 pounds per square inch on the drilling equipment. One expert likened the situation to hellfire; hardened steel equipment often came back to the surface pitted and scarred. During its drilling work, the Bertha Rogers struck molten sulfur, and corrosive pockets of hydrogen sulfide were also encountered, which could make it hazardous to the crews working the rig. How to cope with these conditions was one of the major challenges to building a gas industry in the Anadarko Basin. The Bertha Rogers No. 1 itself had to be capped back at a much shallower depth of approximately 14,000 feet—the pipe and other equipment could not long stand the strain of 6 miles under.

Like its predecessors, the Bertha Rogers as a business venture was a losing proposition. It cost an estimated $7 million but yielded relatively little gas. Some observers classified it as an ultra-deep dry hole.

Yet Hefner claimed the well was worth it for the valuable information it provided regarding the geological formations and other promising signs of natural gas deposits at that great depth or greater. He and his partners were encouraged to continue, but first they knew that the federal price controls, which stacked the deck against ultra-deep production, had to be changed.

By the late 1970s, government officials and Congress were becoming receptive to finding new sources of energy as well as alternatives to foreign oil. Hefner lobbied personally in Washington for a modification of the price controls—some called it a loophole—that would allow gas found below 15,000 feet to be sold at prices three to four times higher than other gas on the market. When the measure was passed as part of the Natural Gas Policy Act of 1978, the Anadarko Basin boom was on in earnest.

It was Oklahoma's last great energy boom to date. Rising oil prices had already brought a surge of interested companies to towns like Elk City, the population of which rose by thousands over the course of the decade as workers eager for high blue-collar wages poured into the region. Their shiny new pickup trucks sported bumper stickers declaring pride in being "oil field trash." Hefner later estimated that companies like his had invested $10–$15 billion in ultra-deep drilling in the Anadarko Basin between 1978 and 1983, much of it financed by bank loans. The bet was safe, because prosperity seemed as limitless as the vast reservoirs of gas.

Of course, it could not last. As supplies outstripped demand, and as consumers switched to less expensive fuels, what inevitably became known as the "gas bubble" drove down prices and sent hundreds of energy-related companies into bankruptcy. By 1983 it was all over, and nationally the financial fallout continued with the collapse of Oklahoma City's infamous Penn Square Bank. Hefner's own business had creditors' claims against it of $125 million in that year. He nevertheless remembered the days of the Bertha Rogers No. 1 fondly and remained optimistic about the future of the Anadarko Basin.

His optimism proved to be well placed. Production in the basin picked up again by the late 1990s. Advances in technology had decreased drilling times by as much as two-thirds, which helped to contain costs. As of 2002, Oklahoma's deep wells had produced over six trillion cubic feet of gas, with another sixteen trillion still estimated to be in the ground. Ironically, by 2004, natural gas had gradually passed crude oil to become the state's most valuable energy commodity—a far cry from the era when it was vented into the atmosphere as waste by drillers looking for black gold.

THE KAREN SILKWOOD MYSTERY

- 1974 -

Crescent

EVERYONE KNOWS THAT KAREN SILKWOOD WAS MURDERED on her way to deliver incriminating evidence to a reporter during the night of November 13, 1974. Or was she? Silkwood's story has been made famous by movies, documentaries, books, and innumerable newspaper and magazine articles. But will it ever be known with certainty why she crashed her car on that cold evening along Highway 74?

Silkwood, a twenty-eight-year-old Texas native, had moved to Oklahoma in 1972. She quickly found a job as a lab technician at the Kerr-McGee Corporation's Cimarron Facility, located near Crescent. There the company had contracted to fashion plutonium into fuel rods for a new generation of experimental nuclear reactors. Silkwood became active in the Oil, Chemical, and Atomic Workers Union, and she began to question safety and quality control procedures at the plant. Among other problems, she claimed that the company was doctoring X-rays that showed shoddy welds in its fuel rods, posing a risk to public safety. Silkwood allegedly had documented evidence about the cover-up that she was bringing to the *New York Times* reporter on the night of her car wreck.

The mystery actually began three weeks earlier. It was discovered that Silkwood had become faintly contaminated with plutonium, but the exact source was unknown. On October 22, radiation was detected in a urine sample that Silkwood was routinely required to furnish. On November 5, plutonium was detected on Silkwood's hands, and steps were taken to decontaminate her. Health officers from Kerr-McGee accompanied Silkwood to her apartment and there found significant radiation levels in the bathroom and kitchen, including on a package of bologna as well as on her roommate's body. The apartment was cleaned and decontaminated, with many of the women's belongings sealed into barrels. The officials also arranged for Silkwood, her boyfriend, and her roommate (who was a coworker) to travel to Los Alamos National Laboratory for further testing on November 11. Silkwood's friends showed clean on the tests, but Silkwood herself was found to have significant, though nonlethal, amounts of plutonium in her lungs.

The three friends returned to Oklahoma on November 12, and Silkwood and her roommate went to work as usual the following day. However, they were prohibited from working with radioactive substances pending further investigation of the earlier exposures. Silkwood went to a union meeting following work, then left in her car, a white Honda Civic, at approximately 7:00 P.M. At 8:05 P.M., the state highway patrol received a report of a car off the road several miles south of Crescent on Highway 74. Silkwood's Honda had veered off the road and traveled along the shoulder for a hundred yards or so before striking a concrete culvert. Silkwood died at the scene.

The highway patrol considered the wreck an accident, probably caused when Silkwood fell asleep at the wheel. An autopsy was requested from the state medical examiner, but since Silkwood's body was contaminated by plutonium, specialists were brought in from Los Alamos to assist. They concluded that she had indeed been exposed to plutonium very recently, based on how far the substance had moved through her internal organs. They also found that she had a large dose of the sedative methaqualone in her stomach, far more than enough to cause sleepiness.

Silkwood's family, friends, and supporters were suspicious of such findings. They wondered why someone would take a strong sedative before driving, and particularly before an important meeting with a reporter. In fact, the Justice Department determined that the evidence for an asleep-at-the-wheel accident was inconclusive. They thought it strange that Silkwood's car had remained on the shoulder for such a long distance, as if she were being prevented from coming back onto the highway. There were witnesses who saw odd dents on the rear fender of her car, dents that could not be accounted for by the head-on impact. And, they wondered, where were the documents that Karen was carrying to show the reporter?

Yet theories of a conspiracy to murder Silkwood were called into question by other facts and circumstances. She had been involved in another single-car accident in the same vehicle on October 31, reportedly swerving off the road to miss hitting a cow. She was a habitual user of prescription tranquilizers, suffered from depression, and was under considerable physical and mental stress at the time of her death. Moreover, if Silkwood's employer was bent on ridding itself of her, why were extensive medical tests arranged for her in the days before her death, and why was she prevented from working with radioactive substances during what turned out to be her last shift?

In retrospect, setting aside the issue of what caused her death, it appears that Silkwood was right to be concerned about health and safety problems at the Cimarron plant. Kerr-McGee was cited for at least seventy-five "minor" violations by federal regulators, who were generally friendly and lenient with the nuclear industry. Contamination of workers at Crescent seems to have been a recurring problem. Workers were inadequately trained, and radiation monitoring was lax, as was security. There were stories of fuel pellets from an adjoining uranium facility that were brought home in workers' pockets and that eventually found their way into the hands of curious children. Reports were published nationally on the alarming amounts of plutonium unaccounted for in routine inventories. Opened in 1970, the Cimarron plutonium plant closed in 1975.

In late 1976, Karen Silkwood's family filed a civil lawsuit against Kerr-McGee, alleging conspiracy and negligence in the plutonium contamination of their daughter. On May 18, 1979, after an eleven-week federal trial conducted against the backdrop of the Three Mile Island nuclear accident, the Silkwoods won a jury award of $10.5 million. This decision was later reversed on appeal by the company, but the U.S. Supreme Court then ruled in the Silkwood family's favor. A retrial was averted in 1986 when the two sides agreed to an out-of-court settlement of $1.38 million.

Karen Silkwood became a martyr for the burgeoning anti-nuclear movement, which equated her name with the dangers of nuclear technology. Ironically, a 1985 report in the *New York Times* indicated that the fuel rods Silkwood had warned about had performed normally in a reactor at Hanford, Washington. Yet within weeks of that report, Kerr-McGee was forced to close its uranium plant in Gore, Oklahoma, after an accident left one worker dead and dozens injured. Thereafter the company decided to abandon the nuclear fuel-processing business altogether.

900-FOOT JESUS

- 1980 -

Tulsa

ON MAY 1, 1955, ANNA WILLIAMS OF WICHITA FALLS, Texas, was watching a revival led by evangelist Oral Roberts, broadcast into her living room from his famous "tent cathedral." Williams, confined to a wheelchair, was afflicted with polio and spinal problems. She listened as Roberts told his home viewers that they could experience the healing power of prayer through their television sets. Williams placed a hand over her heart while she prayed along with him. Immediately afterward she asked her husband to help her stand, and soon she was walking, then dancing, around the room. The story made news nationwide.

Oral Roberts's City of Faith Medical and Research Center arose out of such stories, the deep evangelical belief in personal prayer and miracles. Opened in south Tulsa in November 1981, its three golden towers stood twenty, thirty, and sixty stories tall—the latter by some measures was the tallest building in Oklahoma. The soaring architecture of the City of Faith was an expression of Roberts's own sense of mission. He had moved his ministry into the age of television in the mid-1950s, reaching millions more people than the old-fashioned revivals could. He had built Oral Roberts University during the following decade, the idea for which had come to him through a divine message, ordering him to train missionaries for the farthest reaches of the earth. The City of Faith itself was the result of another divine visitation, according to Roberts. In 1977, while he and his wife were on a Palm Springs retreat, mourning the loss of their daughter earlier that year in a plane crash, Roberts heard the voice of God outline to him the details of the City of Faith complex, including a sculpture of two giant hands that would symbolize prayer and medicine coming together for healing.

Those bronze hands also represented how Oral Roberts blended together the sacred and the secular, the godly and the worldly, in all of his enterprises. The City of Faith would emphasize prayer and spirituality, but would have the best doctors and the latest technology as well. Such things cost money, especially on the scale that Roberts was planning. He expected as many as a million patients per year to visit the center, which would have over two million square feet of floor space. The hospital portion would have 777 beds (a biblically significant number). The twenty-story tower would be a research building. The central building of sixty stories, the clinic, would have as many as 300 doctors working in it. The four-story base of the complex would be 500 feet by 300 feet, requiring over 10 miles of wall partitions to construct its laboratories and examining rooms. The "Praying Hands," touted as the largest cast bronze sculpture in the world, would reach sixty feet high, arching over one end of an 800-foot artificial stream representing the heavenly river of life. The total cost of the project was estimated between $250 million and $400 million— a huge amount to raise, even for the seasoned Oral Roberts.

The groundbreaking took place on January 24, 1978, Roberts's birthday, but soon a fierce legal battle developed over the proposed center. Opponents claimed that a new hospital in Tulsa was unnecessary and would adversely affect medical costs. As construction progressed anyway, the case went up to the Oklahoma Supreme Court, which in April 1981 ruled in Roberts's favor. This was fortunate, because builders had already achieved the maximum height of the clinic tower nearly a year earlier. Yet the interior was largely unfinished, an empty shell.

It was in this context of legal challenges and financial worries that Roberts revealed to his followers that he had experienced another divine vision. In a September 1980 magazine article, he wrote that on May 25, 1980, the Son of God had appeared to him during a visit to the City of Faith construction site. The clinic tower was over 600 feet tall, but Jesus loomed over it—at least 900 feet in height. According to Roberts, Jesus put His hands under the foundation of the complex and lifted it, remarking how easy it was for Him. Roberts told Jesus that the project was out of money, and Jesus exhorted him to rouse his followers to make more contributions. Roberts claimed that he was greatly moved by the whole experience and reinvigorated. An illustration showing Jesus holding the City of Faith accompanied the article, as did a coupon that would commit followers to fifteen months of tithes.

When reports of the 900-foot Jesus spread in the mainstream media, Roberts was ridiculed; in his own view, he was persecuted. His story of the vision proved to be an effective fundraising tool, immediately bringing in as much as $5 million from his so-called prayer partners. And although Roberts claimed to have suffered persecution, the image of a giant Jesus hefting the City of Faith continued to be printed in his publications for years thereafter.

The City of Faith Medical and Research Center officially opened on November 1, 1981, but it never lived up to its billing.

On opening day, only a few floors of the clinic and hospital were occupied, and center officials admitted that the complex was still at least 80 percent unfinished on the inside. The hospital had been approved for only 294 beds rather than 777, and as late as 1984, just 130 were operational. Only three floors of the research tower were in use at that time.

Year after year, the complex lurched from one financial crisis to another, nursed along by Roberts's loyal supporters, but never on sound footing. In an August 1984 article, Roberts told of another encounter with Jesus he had while staying at the City of Faith for surgery. He recalled the earlier sighting of the 900-foot Jesus for his readers, but now, perhaps chastened by the public reaction, Roberts wrote that the Jesus who stood at the end of his hospital bed was the size of a man. Again Jesus gave encouragement about the future of the City of Faith, and offered Roberts the services of an angel to go out and bring in more patients. He promised blessings to those who in turn blessed the City of Faith with their support.

Visions aside, Roberts announced the closing of the City of Faith Medical Center on September 14, 1989. The complex had run a deficit every year of its existence. The droves of out-of-state patients had never materialized. Records showed that only 27,000 patients were treated at the facility between 1981 and 1988—far from the million per year that Roberts had prophesied. By the time of the closing, donations had dried up as well to less than 1 percent of what they had been in the opening year.

Since the early 1990s, the City of Faith has enjoyed an afterlife of sorts as an office complex, the largest in Oklahoma. It was renamed the CityPlex Towers in 1993 and has been considerably more successful as a commercial venture than it was as a medical establishment. Into the late 1990s, the research tower was still mostly unfinished, but in an interesting twist of fate, the thirty-story tower came to house an orthopedic hospital, and other health-related businesses have also used the site. Millions of dollars were spent renovating the buildings over the years, including removal of the cross-designs that once adorned the three golden towers. And in 1991, after they were relocated to the campus of Oral Roberts University, the "Praying Hands" were no longer there to uplift the City of Faith.

TERROR IN THE HEARTLAND

- 1995 -

Oklahoma City

THE INCONGRUITY OF IT STRUCK PEOPLE BEFORE the enormity did. As the shockwave raced outward across city streets and into the countryside beyond, some thought it was a thunderclap, though the sky was clear and sunny. Maybe a sonic boom? Or a gas main? Windows rattled even in towns far away, and seismometers near Norman recorded the event—it must be an earthquake. Everywhere it was heard or felt, people looked up, paused, checked out their windows: what they saw was a different world. It was Wednesday, April 19, 1995, the day of the Oklahoma City bombing.

Around a quarter past ten o'clock on that morning, a highway patrolman stopped an old yellow Mercury heading north on Interstate 35 without a license tag. The young man driving the car admitted that he was carrying a concealed weapon, and the officer took him into custody without incident. Two days later, the young man, soon to be revealed to the nation as Timothy McVeigh, was connected to the rental of a truck that had been traced to the bombing. McVeigh and his accomplice in the crime, Terry Nichols, envisioned themselves as patriots beset on all sides by government oppression and tyranny, but they had been tripped up by routine law enforcement.

Not quite devoted enough to his cause to sacrifice his own life, McVeigh was hoping to escape back into the obscurity from which he and Nichols had plotted the bombing in the preceding months. Using a variety of aliases, the two men had assembled the ingredients of a massive bomb mostly from ordinary items available in the farm co-ops and hardware stores of central Kansas. Ammonium nitrate fertilizer and fuel-oil were mixed together in large plastic drums, which were arranged in the rear of a panel truck to direct a blast with maximum effect. The bomb weighed as much as 4,800 pounds, and it yielded an explosion the equivalent of two tons of TNT.

On April 19, as hundreds of men, women, and children were settling in for the day at the Alfred P. Murrah Federal Building in downtown Oklahoma City, McVeigh parked the truck at the front doors with fuse lit and walked to his getaway car. At 9:02 A.M., the bomb detonated. Moving at thousands of feet per second, the shockwave shattered the beams and columns of the building, causing floor after floor, nine in all, to collapse on top of each other. Ten other buildings nearby also collapsed, while twenty-five more sustained damage. Three hundred additional buildings had windows blown out. Glass and other debris rained down over the area for minutes after the explosion occurred. Numerous burning cars by the Murrah building poured black smoke into the air, adding to the sense of pandemonium.

Emergency responders quickly converged on the scene of devastation. For the first time in its history, the entire Oklahoma City Fire Department was called into action. Firemen, police, and medical workers searched urgently through the rubble for the dead, the wounded, and the survivors—though the process would actually take days to complete and would require the assistance of rescue teams from across the country. The final toll in the Murrah and surrounding buildings was 850 injured and 168 killed, including nineteen children. The image of fireman Chris Fields cradling the little body of Baylee Almon was one never to be forgotten.

Just as ordinary materials were mixed together to create this horror, so too were ordinary things—a chainlink fence, an old elm tree—imbued with sacred meaning in an attempt to redeem it. For many weeks the fence around the bombsite served as a makeshift memorial, where teddy bears were left and notes of grief were pinned. Oklahomans, in fact, were overwhelmed by the outpouring of sympathy and support that came from around the world. In all, over 12,000 people helped with rescue and recovery. The city school system alone received over 400,000 cards, letters, and pictures, mostly from children.

In 1997, Timothy McVeigh was convicted of the bombing and in the deaths of eight federal agents whose offices had been in the Murrah building. He was executed, unremorseful, in 2001. Terry Nichols was convicted in 1997 of lesser federal charges and sentenced to life in prison without parole. He was subsequently tried on state charges and convicted in 2004 of 161 counts of first-degree murder, again receiving the sentence of life without parole.

The Oklahoma City National Memorial was dedicated on the former site of the Murrah building in 2001. There, rows of empty chairs sit beside a reflecting pool and convey a sense of peacefulness and loss. The memorial builders went to great lengths to incorporate into the design the old elm that had come to be known as the Survivor Tree. Somehow it had withstood the blast, the fires, and the final demolition of the broken shell of the Murrah building. Special piers supporting part of the memorial's architecture were excavated by hand to avoid damaging the tree's roots, and an irrigation system was installed. Cuttings from the Survivor Tree were sent to growers all across America, ensuring that it would live on for future generations.

The Oklahoma City bombing echoed back to the land-run cannonshot of April 22, 1889, which founded the city, for it was equally a definitive event in the city's history. Oklahoma City became a place where such things could happen, joining world-weary New York, Belfast, and Beirut. Yet Oklahoma City has responded to this sobering moment by devoting itself with renewed energy to what amounts to a large-scale reinvention of the downtown area. A new library, baseball stadium, and art museum have been constructed since the bombing, along with many other municipal improvements. A new federal building has also risen from the cityscape, with a view of the memorial. Some employees found it too painful to work there, showing that the process of healing was still going on for many survivors and loved ones. The Oklahoma City bombing was an event that had no end to its aftermath.

GO TO THE CROSS

- 1999 -

Moore

As darkness descended on the vast scene of wreckage left in the wake of the May 3, 1999, tornado outbreak in central Oklahoma, rescuers pointed spotlights on the white multi-story cross adorning the First Baptist Church of Moore. The church had become an emergency center despite being damaged itself. The storm had come and gone in the early evening, and it grew dark very quickly in the area of devastation. Streetlights and utility poles had gone the way of everything else in the tornado's path, and the impromptu beacon stood out in the night. *Go to the cross,* people were told when they asked for help. *Go to the cross.*

In Oklahoma, May is the cruelest month, although April and June will do about as well. May is when tornadoes are most likely to form. Usually they come in the late afternoon or early evening. Often they move from the southwest to the northeast. Weathermen can make generalizations about tornadic behavior based on statistics, but they cannot say where the next one will hit until it is almost upon you. They call it the "lead-time." In Oklahoma City on May 3, 1999, the lead-time was eighteen minutes.

If Tornado Alley can be said to have a capital, it would be Oklahoma City. It is a huge sprawling target that lies in the heart of an area that, when represented on colored maps of historic tornado strikes, is usually deep red. One recent count tallied at least 112 tornadoes between 1880 and 2003 in the greater metropolitan area. On seventeen occasions during that period, the city was struck by multiple twisters on the same day. Eight tornadoes rated as F4 ("devastating") and one as F5 (that of May 3) have been verified as occurring in the city area over those 123 years. The May 3rd tornado followed much the same path as an F4 storm that hit on April 25, 1893, and killed thirty-one people. An F5 tornado results in "incredible" damage, to use the scientific definition. Some observers wanted to rate the May 3 storm as an "F6," or "inconceivable" tornado, based on its world-record maximum wind speed of 318 mph—the very tip-top of the F5 scale.

As many as sixty tornadoes raked thirty Oklahoma counties during the afternoon and evening of that day, but the one that first descended from the clouds near Amber was singular from the start. As it passed through Bridge Creek and Newcastle as an F4/F5, it was a mile wide. It weakened and shrank somewhat before restrengthening as it roared across Moore and south Oklahoma City, crossing interstates and expressways with a diameter now of one-half to three-quarters of a mile. The tornado turned then toward Del City and Midwest City, still at F4 level and with a width of up to one-half mile until, quite rapidly, it dissipated. It had been on the ground from 6:26 P.M. to 7:48 P.M.—a relatively long lifespan for a tornado. It must have seemed much longer to those unlucky enough to be under it.

Homes, apartments, businesses, churches, and schools were destroyed, many of them simply obliterated. Some analysts compared the maximum wind speed of the storm to the shockwave of a nuclear explosion. Thirty-six people lost their lives in the metro area alone, including twelve in the small community of Bridge Creek. All that could be said in the aftermath regarding loss of life was that it could have been much worse, but for the lead-time that advanced technology had provided. Statewide, forty-four individuals died and over 800 were injured, and the tally of the property damage made the May 3 tornado the most destructive in history—a true "storm of the century." More than 8,000 buildings had been damaged or destroyed, along with 20,000-plus automobiles, all with an estimated value of over $1 billion.

"Incredible" is the best word to describe the damage wrought by the storm. Witnesses told of empty school buses being picked up and thrown the length of two football fields. The cars of a full parking lot were swept onto the second story of a nearby hotel, pancaked one on top of the other. Perhaps the most terrifying story to emerge from that day concerned the fate of a twenty-three-year-old Seminole woman, who was swept away by the wind while seeking shelter under a highway overpass with her husband and children. Her remains were not found for several days.

The May 3 tornado outbreak also had its oddities and miracles. Not only a lot of pets but also a lot of guns, it seems, became separated from their owners as a consequence of the storm; searchers collected dozens of firearms from the debris that had literally fallen from the sky. In the days following the outbreak, warnings were issued to farmers to beware of pink insulation blown into their pastures, which was potentially deadly to grazing cattle. One farmer near a flattened strip mall in the Stroud area lost three animals to insulation, until volunteers filled over 300 garbage bags from his land. Most poignant of all, however, was the story of the sheriff's deputy in Grady County, who picked up what appeared to be a rag doll lying under a tree in the immediate aftermath. It was a missing baby who had been blown from her mother's arms. To the deputy's relief, the baby, at first silent and caked with mud, began to cry.

The story of the baby might have made a gentle, uplifting epilogue to the May 3 storm of the century, but nature makes history volatile in Oklahoma. On May 8, 2003, a series of tornadoes plowed an almost identical path across the Oklahoma City area. In one particular subdivision, some victims who had lost their homes in 1999 lost them again in 2003; some had relocated several blocks away, and the tornado still found them. A few survivors announced their intentions to move. Others vowed to rebuild.

OKLAHOMA FACTS AND TRIVIA

Oklahoma's land area is 69,919 square miles; it is larger than any state east of the Mississippi River.

The landscape of Oklahoma, which includes swamps, forests, prairies, and mesas, has been rated by the Environmental Protection Agency as one of the most diverse in the United States.

Three of Oklahoma's principal mountain ranges—the Ouachitas, the Arbuckles, and the Wichitas—are geologically considered to be part of the Appalachian mountain chain of the eastern United States.

The highest point in Oklahoma is Black Mesa, at 4,973 ft. The lowest point, almost 500 miles to the southeast, is 287 ft., near Idabel.

Cimarron County is the only county in the U.S. that borders on five states—Oklahoma, Texas, New Mexico, Kansas, and Colorado.

The state flower is mistletoe.

The state tree is the redbud.

The state bird is the scissor-tailed flycatcher.

The state meal includes chicken-fried steak, pecan pie, fried okra, and black-eyed peas.

The state rock is the rose rock, the barite variety found in very few places on earth.

The state capital is Oklahoma City.

The population of Oklahoma is over 3.5 million (2003).

Oklahoma, although nearly 500 miles inland, has its own ocean port—the Tulsa Port of Catoosa on the McClellan-Kerr Arkansas River Navigational System.

Construction of the Oklahoma State Capitol, which began in 1914, was not complete until 2002, when a dome was finally added. It is also the only state capitol with an oil well on its grounds.

Thirty-nine different Native American tribes and nations have their headquarters in Oklahoma. Over 280,000 Native Americans lived in Oklahoma as of 2003.

Oklahoma attained statehood on November 16, 1907, as the forty-sixth state in the union.

The state motto is *Labor Omnia Vincit* ("Labor Conquers All Things").

Oklahoma's nickname is the Sooner State.

BIBLIOGRAPHY

Preface

"Food on the Fly." *Daily Oklahoman,* April 10, 2002.

Latham, Lisa Moricoli. "Southern Governors Declare War on Divorce." www.salon.com/mwt/feature/2000/01/24/divorce.

Lindsey, William, and Mark Silk, eds. *Religion and Public Life in the Southern Crossroads: Showdown States.* Walnut Creek, Calif.: AltaMira Press, 2005.

Morris, John W., Charles R. Goins, and Edwin C. McReynolds. *Historical Atlas of Oklahoma.* 2nd ed. Norman, Okla.: University of Oklahoma Press, 1976.

"Neustadt International Prize for Literature." *World Literature Today.* www.ou.edu/worldlit/neustadt/.

"Oklahoma Ties." *Daily Oklahoman,* February 16, 2005.

U.S. Department of Commerce and Labor. *Statistical Abstract of the United States.* Washington, D.C.: Government Printing Office, 1911.

Old Paint—8,000 B.C.

Bement, Leland C. *Bison Hunting at Cooper Site: Where Lightning Bolts Drew Thundering Herds.* Norman, Okla.: University of Oklahoma Press, 1999.

Bement, Leland C., Marian Hyman, Michael E. Zolensky, and Brian J. Carter. "A Painted Skull from the Cooper Site: A Folsom Bison Kill in NW Oklahoma." *Current Research in the Pleistocene* 14 (1997): 6–9.

Carter, Brian J., and Leland C. Bement. "Geoarchaeology of the Cooper Site, Northwest Oklahoma: Evidence for Multiple Folsom Bison Kills." *Geoarchaeology: An International Journal* 18, no. 1 (January 2003): 115–27.

Gilbert, Claudette Marie, and Robert L. Brooks. *From Mounds to Mammoths: A Field Guide to Oklahoma Prehistory.* Norman, Okla.: University of Oklahoma Press, 2000.

Rune or Ruse?—A.D. 1012

Farley, Cynthia. "The Oklahoma Runestones." Chap. 9 in *In Plain Sight: Old World Records in Ancient America.* Columbus, Ga.: ISAC Press, 1994. www2.privatei.com/~bartjean/chap9.htm.

———. "A Response to Dr. Lee Woodard's Theory on the Heavener Runestone." *The Oklahoma Traveler: The Mystery of the Heavener Runestone* (n.d.). www.kotv.com.

Farris, David A. *Mysterious Oklahoma: Eerie True Tales from the Sooner State.* Edmond, Okla.: Little Bruce, 1995.

Landsverk, O. G. *Runic Records of the Norsemen in America.* New York: Erik J. Friis, 1974.

Money, Jack. "State OKs Investigation of Runestone." *Daily Oklahoman,* July 18, 2003.

———. "Ultraviolet Light to Play Heavener Runestone Role." *Daily Oklahoman,* August 17, 2003.

Mongé, Alf, and O. G. Landsverk. *Norse Medieval Cryptography in Runic Carvings.* Glendale, Calif.: Norseman Press, 1967.

Woodard, Lee W. "The Heavener Rune Stone Explained as James (Jimmy, Gemme) Hiens' Secret La Salle Monument and Historical Marker." *The Oklahoma Traveler: The Mystery of the Heavener Runestone* (n.d.). www.kotv.com.

That Fatal Country—1834

Allgood, Samuel Y. "Historic Spots and Actions in the Washita Valley Up to 1870." *Chronicles of Oklahoma* 5, no. 2 (June 1927): 221–33.

Catlin, George. *Letters and Notes on the Manners, Customs, and Conditions of North American Indians.* Vol. 2. New York: Dover, 1973.

Hoig, Stan. *Beyond the Frontier: Exploring the Indian Country.* Norman, Okla.: University of Oklahoma Press, 1998.

After the Tears—1846

Foreman, Grant. *Indian Removal: The Emigration of the Five Civilized Tribes of Indians.* Norman, Okla.: University of Oklahoma Press, 1972.

McLoughlin, William G. *After the Trail of Tears: The Cherokees' Struggle for Sovereignty, 1839–1880.* Chapel Hill, N.C.: University of North Carolina Press, 1993.

Thornton, Russell. *The Cherokees: A Population History.* Lincoln, Neb.: University of Nebraska Press, 1990.

A Second Trail of Tears—1861

Debo, Angie. *The Road to Disappearance: A History of the Creek Indians*. Norman, Okla.: University of Oklahoma Press, 1941.

Hoig, Stanley W. *The Cherokees and Their Chiefs*. Fayetteville, Ark.: University of Arkansas Press, 1998.

Meserve, John Bartlett. "Chief Opothleyahola." *Chronicles of Oklahoma* 9, no. 4 (December 1931): 439–53.

Wilson, Steve. *Oklahoma Treasures and Treasure Tales*. Norman, Okla.: University of Oklahoma Press, 1989.

The Trail That Built a Kingdom—1867

Gard, Wayne. *The Chisholm Trail*. Norman, Okla.: University of Oklahoma Press, 1979.

Hoig, Stan. *Jesse Chisholm: Ambassador of the Plains*. Norman, Okla.: University of Oklahoma, 1991.

McCoy, Joseph G. *Historic Sketches of the Cattle Trade of the West and Southwest*. Kansas City, Mo.: Ramsey, Millett & Hudson, 1874. www.kancoll.org/books/mccoy/index.html.

Skaggs, Jimmy M., ed. *Ranch and Range in Oklahoma*. Oklahoma City: Oklahoma Historical Society, 1978.

Worcester, Donald E. "Chisholm Trail." *The Handbook of Texas Online*. www.tsha.utexas.edu/handbook/online/articles/CC/ayc2.html.

————. *The Chisholm Trail: High Road of the Cattle Kingdom*. Lincoln, Neb.: University of Nebraska Press, 1980.

Custer's Dress Rehearsal—1868

Brill, Charles J. *Custer, Black Kettle, and the Fight on the Washita.* Norman, Okla.: University of Oklahoma Press, 2002.

Connell, Evan S. *Son of the Morning Star: Custer and the Little Bighorn.* San Francisco: North Point Press, 1984.

Greene, Jerome A. *Washita: The U.S. Army and the Southern Cheyennes, 1867–1869.* Norman, Okla.: University of Oklahoma Press, 2004.

Hoig, Stan. *The Battle of the Washita.* Lincoln, Neb.: University of Nebraska Press, 1979.

Indomitable—1873

Gibson, Arrell Morgan. *The Chickasaws.* Norman, Okla.: University of Oklahoma Press, 1981.

———. *The Kickapoos: Lords of the Middle Border.* Norman, Okla.: University of Oklahoma Press, 1963.

Herring, Joseph B. "Cultural and Economic Resilience Among the Kickapoo Indians of the Southwest." *Great Plains Quarterly* 6 (Fall 1986): 263–75.

Hitchcock, Ethan Allen. *A Traveler in Indian Territory: The Journal of Ethan Allen Hitchcock, Late Major-General in the United States Army.* Edited by Grant Foreman. Norman, Okla.: University of Oklahoma Press, 1996.

Boomer Sooner—1890

Baldwin, Kathlyn. *The 89ers: Oklahoma Land Rush of 1889.* Oklahoma City: Western Heritage Books, 1981.

"The Chief Boomer Shot." *New York Times,* April 5, 1890.

Hoig, Stan. *The Oklahoma Land Run of 1889.* Oklahoma City: Oklahoma Historical Society, 1989.

Thompson, John. *Closing the Frontier: Radical Response in Oklahoma, 1889–1923.* Norman, Okla.: University of Oklahoma Press, 1986.

Welsh, Carol H. "Deadly Games: The Struggle for a Quarter-section of Land." *Chronicles of Oklahoma* 52, no. 1 (Spring 1994): 36–51.

Dead or Alive, Preferably Dead—1892

Burton, Arthur T. *Black, Red, and Deadly: Black and Indian Gunfighters of the Indian Territories.* Austin, Tex.: Eakin Press, 1991.

Cherokee Nation Cultural Resource Center. "Ned Christie." Tahlequah, Okla., 2005. www.cherokee.org/CULTURE/History Page.asp?ID=59.

Shirley, Glenn. *Heck Thomas: Frontier Marshal.* Norman, Okla.: University of Oklahoma Press, 1981.

Speer, Bonnie Stahlman. *The Killing of Ned Christie, Cherokee Outlaw.* Norman, Okla.: Reliance Press, 2000.

Steele, Phillip. *The Last Cherokee Warriors: Zeke Proctor, Ned Christie.* Gretna, La.: Pelican Publishing Company, 1974.

Taking Bill Doolin, Twice—1896

Nix, Evett Dumas. *Oklahombres: Particularly the Wilder Ones.* Lincoln, Neb.: University of Nebraska Press, 1993.

Shirley, Glenn. *Heck Thomas: Frontier Marshal.* Norman, Okla.: University of Oklahoma Press, 1981.

————. *West of Hell's Fringe: Crime, Criminals, and the Federal Peace Officer in Oklahoma Territory, 1889–1907.* Norman, Okla.: University of Oklahoma Press, 1978.

Gala Day—1905

Collings, Ellsworth and Alma Miller England. *The 101 Ranch.* Norman, Okla.: University of Oklahoma Press, 1971.

101 Ranch Oldtimers Association. *101 Ranch Home Page.* www.kaycounty.info/101_Ranch/101_frame.htm.

Wallis, Michael. *The Real Wild West: The 101 Ranch and the Creation of the American West.* New York: St. Martin's Press, 1999.

Buffalo Comeback—1907

"Buffaloes Eat Trash and Die." *Daily Oklahoman,* April 4, 1978.

Dary, David A. *The Buffalo Book: The Full Saga of the American Animal.* Chicago: Sage Books, 1974.

Hagan, William T. *Quanah Parker, Comanche Chief.* Norman, Okla.: University of Oklahoma Press, 1993.

Hornaday, William T. *Our Vanishing Wildlife: Its Extermination and Preservation.* New York: Arno Press, 1970.

Lott, Dale F. *American Bison: A Natural History.* Berkeley: University of California Press, 2002.

"A Magnificent Game Preserve." *Daily Oklahoman,* September 2, 1906.

"A New National Buffalo Herd." *Science* 26, no. 669 (October 25, 1907): 563–64.

"New York Zoological Society Saved Buffalo Herd Just Fifty Years Ago." *Daily Oklahoman,* October 17, 1957.

"The Refuge Herd." *Daily Oklahoman,* September 12, 1954.

"State Buffalo Herd to Be Cut in Half." *Daily Oklahoman,* September 19, 1971.

U.S. Department of Agriculture. National Agricultural Statistics Service. "Other Animals and Animal Products—Inventory and Number Sold: 2002 and 1997." Washington, D.C., 2002.www.nass.usda.gov/census/census02/volume1/us/st99_1_030_032.pdf.

U.S. Fish and Wildlife Service. "History of the WR Bison Herd." Washington, D.C., (n.d.) www.fws.gov/southwest/refuges/wichitamountains/bisonhist.html.

"Wichita Buffalo Herd Traced Back to Texas." *Daily Oklahoman,* May 28, 1965.

"Wildlife Refuge Offers Look at Buffalo's Survival." *Daily Oklahoman,* November 17, 1996.

Hold Your Nose and Sign—1907

Bryant, Keith L. *Alfalfa Bill Murray.* Norman, Okla.: University of Oklahoma Press, 1968.

"Constitution Is Denounced By Taft, Before Big Crowd." *Daily Oklahoman,* August 25, 1907.

Goble, Danney. *Progressive Oklahoma: The Making of a New Kind of State.* Norman, Okla.: University of Oklahoma Press, 1980.

"Jibes Roosevelt About Statehood." *Daily Oklahoman*, October 4, 1907.

"Last Saloons Closed Doors Nov. 16, 1907." *Daily Oklahoman*, April 23, 1939.

Morgan, David R., Robert E. England, and George G. Humphreys. *Oklahoma Politics and Policies: Governing the Sooner State*. Lincoln, Neb.: University of Nebraska Press, 1991.

Morgan, H. Wayne, and Anne Hodges Morgan. *Oklahoma: A History*. New York: W. W. Norton, 1984.

Murray, William H. *Memoirs of Governor Murray and True History of Oklahoma*. Vol. 1. Boston: Meador Publishing Company, 1945.

Proposed Constitution of the State of Oklahoma. Washington, D.C.: Government Printing Office, 1907.

Scales, James R., and Danney Goble. *Oklahoma Politics: A History*. Norman, Okla.: University of Oklahoma Press, 1982.

"Scratch of Quill Pen Lets the New State Into Union." *Daily Oklahoman*, November 17, 1907.

Wilson, Charles Morrow. *The Commoner: William Jennings Bryan*. Garden City, N.Y.: Doubleday, 1970.

Land of the Reds—1917

Bissett, Jim. *Agrarian Socialism in America: Marx, Jefferson, and Jesus in the Oklahoma Countryside, 1904–1920*. Norman, Okla.: University of Oklahoma Press, 1999.

———. "Socialism from the Bottom Up: Local Activists and the Socialist Party of Oklahoma, 1900–1920." *Chronicles of Oklahoma* 82, no. 4 (Winter 2004–2005): 388–411.

Sellars, Nigel. "With Folded Arms? or With Squirrel Guns? The IWW and the Green Corn Rebellion." *Chronicles of Oklahoma* 77, no. 2 (Summer 1999): 150–69.

Thompson, John. *Closing the Frontier: Radical Response in Oklahoma, 1889–1923.* Norman, Okla.: University of Oklahoma Press, 1986.

Burning Greenwood—1921

Gillham, Omer. "Race Riot Scholarships Are Awarded." *Tulsa World,* June 11, 2003.

Goble, Danney. *Tulsa! Biography of an American City.* Tulsa: Council Oak Books, 1997.

Hirsch, James S. *Riot and Remembrance: The Tulsa Race War and Its Legacy.* Boston: Houghton Mifflin, 2002.

Jackson, Lawrence. *Ralph Ellison: Emergence of Genius.* New York: John Wiley & Sons, 2002.

Tulsa Race Riot Commission. *Tulsa Race Riot: A Report by the Oklahoma Commission to Study the Tulsa Race Riot of 1921.* Oklahoma City, 2001. www.okhistory.org/trrc/freport.htm.

Wild Mary and No. 1 Stout—1930

Blackburn, Bob L. *Heart of the Promised Land: Oklahoma County, An Illustrated History.* Woodland Hills, Calif.: Windsor Publications, 1982.

"Blowout Rivals North Sea Loss." *Daily Oklahoman,* May 7, 1977.

Boyd, Dan T. "Oklahoma Oil: Past, Present, and Future." *Oklahoma Geology Notes* 62, no. 3 (Fall 2002): 97–106.

"Fiery River Burns Oklahoma Bridges." *New York Times,* November 4, 1930.

"Flee From Flames Near Wild Gusher." *New York Times,* November 2, 1930.

Franks, Kenny A. *The Rush Begins: A History of the Red Fork, Cleveland, and Glenn Pool Oil Fields.* Oklahoma City: Oklahoma Heritage Association, 1984.

Knowles, Ruth Sheldon. *The Greatest Gamblers: The Epic of American Oil Exploration.* Norman, Okla.: University of Oklahoma Press, 1978.

"Oil Firm Head to Pay Claims on Wild Well." *Daily Oklahoman,* November 4, 1930.

"River's Oil Blaze Sets State Agog." *Daily Oklahoman,* November 3, 1930.

"State Guards Against Fires in Oil Field." *Daily Oklahoman,* April 3, 1930.

"Steel Bonnet Is Ready for Unruly Well." *Daily Oklahoman,* April 4, 1930.

"Wild Gusher Capped; Field To Be Cleaned to End Fire Menace." *Daily Oklahoman,* April 5, 1930.

"Wild Gusher May Be Tamed Today." *Daily Oklahoman,* March 31, 1930.

"Wild Gusher Tamed After 11-Day Fight." *Daily Oklahoman,* April 7, 1930.

"Wild Oil Gusher Tamed After 3 Days." *New York Times,* November 3, 1930.

"Wild Well Still Strong." *Daily Oklahoman,* April 2, 1930.

"Workmen Due to Cap Wild Gusher Today." *Daily Oklahoman,* November 2, 1930.

King Tut's Tomb, Oklahoma-Style—1933

Brown, James A. *The Spiro Ceremonial Center: The Archaeology of Arkansas Valley Caddoan Culture in Eastern Oklahoma.* 2 vols. Ann Arbor: Museum of Anthropology, University of Michigan, 1996.

Gilbert, Claudette Marie, and Robert L. Brooks. *From Mounds to Mammoths: A Field Guide to Oklahoma Prehistory.* Norman, Okla.: University of Oklahoma Press, 2000.

Phillips, Philip, and James A. Brown. *Pre-Columbian Shell Engravings From the Craig Mound at Spiro, Oklahoma.* Cambridge, Mass.: Peabody Museum Press, 1978.

Take Me Back to Tulsa—1934

Crow, Kelly. "Oklahoma's Icons: We Tuned In While They Made History." *Oklahoma Today* 49, no. 5 (July/August 1999): 40–49.

Henderson, Bruce. "The Genesis: How Oklahoma Created Country Music." *Oklahoma Today* 49, no. 5 (July/August 1999): 32–39.

McClean, Duncan. *Lone Star Swing: On the Trail of Bob Wills and his Texas Playboys.* New York: W. W. Norton, 1997.

Townsend, Charles R. *San Antonio Rose: The Life and Music of Bob Wills.* Urbana, Ill.: University of Illinois Press, 1986.

Black Sunday—1935

"Dust Storm May Abate Today." *Daily Oklahoman,* April 11, 1935.

Johnson, Vance. *Heaven's Tableland: The Dust Bowl Story.* New York: Da Capo Press, 1974.

Leighton, M. M. "Geology of Soil Drifting on the Great Plains." *The Scientific Monthly,* 47, no. 1 (July 1938): 22–33.

"More Dust, Cold Into State on High Winds." *Daily Oklahoman,* April 15, 1935.

Stallings, Frank L., Jr. *Black Sunday: The Great Dust Storm of April 14, 1935.* Austin, Tex.: Eakin Press, 2001.

Worster, Donald. *Dust Bowl: The Southern Plains in the 1930s.* New York: Oxford University Press, 1979.

Meet the Okies—1939

Blackburn, Bob L. *Heart of the Promised Land: Oklahoma County, An Illustrated History.* Woodland Hills, Calif.: Windsor Publications, 1982.

Gregory, James N. *American Exodus: The Dust Bowl Migration and Okie Culture in California.* New York: Oxford University Press, 1989.

Klein, Joe. *Woody Guthrie: A Life.* New York: Ballantine Books, 1980.

"The 'Okies' Take a Sunnier Road." *New York Times,* May 17, 1942.

Parini, Jay. *John Steinbeck: A Biography.* New York: Henry Holt, 1995.

Shockley, Martin Staples. "The Reception of *The Grapes of Wrath* in Oklahoma." American Literature 15, no. 4 (January 1944): 351–61.

Whisenhunt, Donald W. "'We've Got the Hoover Blues': Oklahoma Transiency in the Days of the Great Depression." In *Hard Times in Oklahoma: The Depression Years,* edited by Kenneth D. Hendrickson Jr., 101–14. Oklahoma City: Oklahoma Historical Society, 1983.

Worster, Donald. *Dust Bowl: The Southern Plains in the 1930s.* New York: Oxford University Press, 1979.

Kate and Angie—1941

Baird, W. David, and Danney Goble. *The Story of Oklahoma.* Norman, Okla.: University of Oklahoma Press, 1994.

Debo, Angie. *And Still the Waters Run: The Betrayal of the Five Civilized Tribes.* Norman, Okla.: University of Oklahoma Press, 1984.

Edmondson, Linda, and Margaret Larason. "Kate Barnard: The Story of a Woman Politician." *Chronicles of Oklahoma* 78, no. 2 (Summer 2000): 160–81.

Lowitt, Richard. "Regionalism at the University of Oklahoma." *Chronicles of Oklahoma* 73, no. 2 (Summer 1995): 150–71.

Reese, Linda Williams. *Women of Oklahoma, 1890–1920.* Norman, Okla.: University of Oklahoma Press, 1997.

Freaks of the Storm—1948

Bedard, Richard. *In the Shadow of the Storm: Stories and Adventures from the Heart of Storm Country.* Norman, Okla.: Gilco Publishing, 1996.

Bluestein, Howard B. *Tornado Alley: Monster Storms of the Great Plains.* New York: Oxford University Press, 1999.

Bradford, Marlene. *Scanning the Skies: A History of Tornado Forecasting.* Norman, Okla.: University of Oklahoma Press, 2001.

Crowder, James L. "Tinker's Twin Twisters of 1948 and the Birth of Tornado Forecasting." *Chronicles of Oklahoma* 78, no. 3 (Fall 2000): 278–95.

Grazulis, Thomas P. *The Tornado: Nature's Ultimate Windstorm.* Norman, Okla.: University of Oklahoma Press, 2001.

———. *Significant Tornadoes, 1880–1989.* Vol. II. St. Johnsbury, Vt.: Environmental Films, 1990.

"Mother and Child Killed in Storm." *Daily Oklahoman,* March 1, 1918.

"Saved Another Woman." *Daily Oklahoman,* May 12, 1905.

"Storm Hits Awful Blow." *Daily Oklahoman,* May 21, 1910.

"Tinker Storm Damage Placed at $20 Million." *Daily Oklahoman,* March 22, 1948.

"When Waiting Is Pain." *Daily Oklahoman,* June 2, 1947.

Wigton, Scott. "Stormin' Norman." *Oklahoma Today* 55, no. 3 (May/June 2005): 57–62.

Visible At Last—1950

Adwan, Alex. "The Man in the Cage." *Tulsa World,* May 22, 1994.

Bittle, William E. "The Desegregated All-White Institution . . . The University of Oklahoma." *Journal of Educational Sociology* 32, no. 6, *Southern Higher Education Since the Gaines Decision: A Twenty Year Review* (February 1959): 275–82.

Fisher, Ada Lois Sipuel. *A Matter of Black and White: The Autobiography of Ada Lois Sipuel Fisher.* Norman, Okla.: University of Oklahoma Press, 1996.

Franklin, Jimmie Lewis. *Journey Toward Hope: A History of Blacks in Oklahoma.* Norman, Okla.: University of Oklahoma Press, 1982.

Luper, Clara. "Behold the Walls." In *"An Oklahoma I Had Never Seen Before": Alternative Views of Oklahoma History,* edited by Davis D. Joyce, 229–48. Norman, Okla.: University of Oklahoma Press, 1994.

Moon, F. D. "Higher Education and Desegregation in Oklahoma." *The Journal of Negro Education* 27, no. 3 (Summer 1958): 300–310.

National Park Service. "Landmarks that Transformed Education: Racial Desegregation in Public Education in the United States." *A National Historic Landmark Theme Study Update* (May 17, 2004): 1–16. www.cr.nps.gov/nhl/Racial%20 Desegregation%20Update.pdf.

"'Reserved for Colored': Memories of Legalized Bigotry at the University of Oklahoma." *The Journal of Blacks in Higher Education,* 31 (Spring 2001): 75.

Black Saturday—1957

Cronley, John. "Irish Snip OU Streak at 47." *Daily Oklahoman,* November 17, 1957.

Dent, Jim. *The Undefeated: The Oklahoma Sooners and the Greatest Winning Streak in College Football.* New York: Thomas Dunne Books, 2001.

Keith, Harold. *Forty-Seven Straight: The Wilkinson Era at Oklahoma.* Norman, Okla.: University of Oklahoma Press, 1984.

"Stunned OU Fans Take Loss Quietly." *Daily Oklahoman,* November 17, 1957.

University of Oklahoma Athletics Dept. "NCAA-Record 47-Game Winning Streak." Norman, Okla., 2004. www.soonersports .com/ViewArticle.dbml?DB_LANG=DB_OEM_ID=300 &&ATCLID=90824.

Way Down Yonder—1972

Baxter, Debby. "Anadarko Basin Gas Reservoir Turns Elk City Into Boom Town." *Daily Oklahoman,* Oct. 16, 1977.

"Burns Flat Gasser Sets New Record." *Daily Oklahoman,* May 12, 1973.

Buss, Dale D. "Hostile Depths Increase Costs of Corrosion for Oil Drillers." *Wall Street Journal,* September 11, 1981.

Lueck, Thomas J. "Bankruptcy for Drillers." *New York Times,* April 26, 1983.

Martin, Douglas. "The Man Who Drills the Deepest Wells." *New York Times,* November 29, 1981.

Morris, John W., ed. *Drill Bits, Picks, and Shovels: A History of Mineral Resources in Oklahoma.* Oklahoma City: Oklahoma Historical Society, 1982.

Nelson, Mary Jo. "Anadarko Basin Boom Has Hardly Begun." *Daily Oklahoman,* October 3, 1982.

Snead, Mark C. *The Economics of Deep Drilling in Oklahoma.* Stillwater, Okla.: Center for Applied Economic Research, 2005. http://economy.okstate.edu/papers/economics%20of%20deep%20drilling.pdf.

Tallent, Becky. "Poison-Gas Danger in Well Blowouts Gets State's Attention." *Daily Oklahoman,* December 27, 1981.

Vandewater, Bob. "Oklahoma Well Shooting for World's Record Depth." *Daily Oklahoman,* February 15, 1981.

The Karen Silkwood Mystery—1974

Curry, Bill, and Paul Wenske. "Silkwood Family Awarded $10.5 Million in Damages." *Washington Post,* May 19, 1979.

Ezell, John Samuel. *Innovations in Energy: The Story of Kerr-McGee.* Norman, Okla.: University of Oklahoma Press, 1979.

"Kerr-McGee Is Cutting Troubled Nuclear Role." *New York Times,* January 6, 1986.

Kohn, Howard. *Who Killed Karen Silkwood?* New York: Summit Books, 1981.

Rashke, Richard. *The Killing of Karen Silkwood: The Story Behind the Kerr-McGee Plutonium Case.* Ithaca, N.Y.: Cornell University Press, 2000.

"Silkwood Epilogue: Fuel-Rod Debate Lingers On." *New York Times,* December 7, 1985.

Triplett, Gene. "Silkwood Trial Still Stirs Emotions." *Daily Oklahoman,* December 16, 1999.

900-Foot Jesus—1980

"City of Faith: A Promise Unfulfilled." *Tulsa World,* September 30, 1989.

Evatt, Robert. "Leases on Life." *Tulsa World,* November 8, 2005.

Harrell, David Edwin, Jr. *Oral Roberts: An American Life.* Bloomington, Ind.: Indiana University Press, 1985.

"ORU to Relocate Praying Hands." *Tulsa World,* May 4, 1991.

Roberts, Oral. "I Must Tell Somebody . . . and I Must Tell You, Dear Partner . . ." *Abundant Life* 24, no. 8 (September 1980): 10–13.

———. "The Master Plan God Has Given Me." *Abundant Life* 21, no. 11 (November 1977): 2–8.

———. "Oral Roberts, open MY City of Faith to the poor and needy." *Abundant Life* 28, no. 8 (August–September 1984): 2–6.

Terror in the Heartland—1995

"After the Blast: Downtown Oklahoma City." www.newsok.com/ features/bombing/images/map_structural_damage.gif.

Hersley, Jon, Larry Tongate, and Bob Burke. *Simple Truths: The Real Story of the Oklahoma City Bombing Investigation.* Oklahoma City: Oklahoma Heritage Association, 2004.

Mlakar, Paul F., Sr., et al. "The Oklahoma City Bombing: Analysis of Blast Damage to the Murrah Building." *Journal of Performance of Constructed Facilities* 12, no. 3 (August 1998): 113–19.

Oklahoma City National Memorial. "Murrah Building Bombing—A Look at Numbers." Oklahoma City, 2005. www.oklahomacity nationalmemorial.org/docs/Murrah%20Bldg%20Numbers.pdf.

Oklahoma Tourism and Recreation Department. *9:02 A.M., April 19, 1995: The Official Record of the Oklahoma City Bombing.* Oklahoma City: Oklahoma Tourism and Recreation Department, 2005.

Pincus, Walter, and George Lardner Jr. "Eight Days in April: Tracing Suspects' Movements in Crucial Period." *Washington Post,* July 3, 1995.

Go to the Cross—1999

Branick, Michael L. "Tornadoes in the Oklahoma City, Oklahoma Area Since 1890." Norman, Okla.: National Weather Service, 2003. www.srh.noaa.gov/oun/tornadodata/okc_tornado.php.

Colberg, Sonya. "Littered Land." *Tulsa World,* May 26, 1999.

Gibbard, Dan. "A Slow, Painful Recovery." *Chicago Tribune,* June 3, 1999.

Monastersky, Richard. "Oklahoma Tornado Sets Wind Record." *Science News* 155, no. 20 (May 15, 1999): 308.

Ode, Kim. "Taking Careful Aim at the Proliferation of Guns." *Minneapolis Star-Tribune,* May 15, 1999.

Ross, Bobby, Jr., and Melissa Nelson. "Storm Damage Evokes Images of War Zone." *Daily Oklahoman,* May 8, 1999.

Tramel, Berry. "Same Song, Second Verse for Some in Moore." *Daily Oklahoman,* May 10, 2003.

Watson, Christy. "Deputy Finds Tiny Survivor of Bridge Creek Tornado." *Daily Oklahoman,* May 8, 1999.

Oklahoma Facts and Trivia

Morris, John W., Charles R. Goins, and Edwin C. McReynolds. *Historical Atlas of Oklahoma.* 2nd ed. Norman, Okla.: University of Oklahoma Press, 1976.

Oklahoma Dept. of Tourism and Recreation. "Oklahoma Fun Facts." Oklahoma City, 2003. www.travelok.com/about/fun_facts.asp.

Roberts, David C. *A Field Guide to Geology: Eastern North America.* Boston: Houghton Mifflin, 1996.

State of Oklahoma. "Oklahoma State Icons." Oklahoma City, 2005. www.state.ok.us/osfdocs/stinfo.html.

U.S. Dept. of Commerce. "Resident Population by Race, Hispanic or Latino Origin, and State: 2003." *Statistical Abstract of the United States: 2004–2005.* Washington, D.C.: U.S. Census Bureau, 2003. www.census.gov/statab/www/sa04aian.pdf.

INDEX

ABOUT THE AUTHOR

Robert L. Dorman was born and raised in Oklahoma and graduated with a degree in history from the University of Oklahoma in 1984. He holds a doctorate in American history from Brown University, Providence, Rhode Island. Dr. Dorman has taught history at such institutions as Harvard University, Brown University, the University of New Mexico, and the University of Oklahoma. He is the author of *Revolt of the Provinces: The Regionalist Movement in America, 1920–1945* and *A Word for Nature: Four Pioneering Environmental Advocates, 1845–1913,* both published by the University of North Carolina Press. In 2005, Dorman was named an Association of Research Libraries Academy fellow by the Catholic University of America, Washington, D.C.